SACRED WISDOM – NATIVE ANERICAN MEDITATIONS, AFFIRMATIONS, AND REFLECTIONS

Embark on a transformative journey of self-discovery and spiritual growth with 'Sacred Wisdom.' This enlightening book offers a year-long exploration of Native American wisdom, providing daily meditations, affirmations, and reflections that draw upon the profound teachings of indigenous cultures. Each day presents a new opportunity to connect with the natural world and its timeless truths, guiding you to find harmony, resilience, and purpose in your life.

Through the quiet strength of mountains, the gentle dance of leaves in the breeze, and the steadfastness of a turtle carrying its home, 'Sacred Wisdom' offers a path to deeper understanding and connection. Whether you seek grounding and stability, inspiration and creativity, or simply a moment of peace in your day, this book will be your companion on a journey of spiritual awakening. Immerse yourself in the wisdom of the land and its people and discover the transformative power of Native American teachings in your daily life.

SACRED WISDOM – NATIVE ANERICAN MEDITATIONS, AFFIRMATIONS, AND REFLECTIONS

January 1

Meditation: As the new year begins, let us embrace the quiet stillness of winter. Imagine the silent snowfall, each flake whispering tranquility. Reflect on the purity of the snow, a clean slate for the coming year.

Affirmation: I am a bearer of peace and renewal. This year unfolds before me full of potential, and I welcome each day with a calm spirit.

Thought: The year starts anew, offering us countless possibilities. Like the cycles of the seasons, we too can renew ourselves, shedding old habits for new growth.

Focus: Renewal and fresh beginnings.

January 2

Meditation: Contemplate the life of a river, constantly flowing, overcoming obstacles with grace and strength. Let the water's journey inspire resilience in your spirit.

Affirmation: I flow with strength and adaptability, embracing life's challenges as opportunities to grow and learn.

Thought: Life is an ever-moving river; by accepting its flow, we find our own path forward.

Focus: Embracing life's continuous flow and changes.

January 3

Meditation: Stand in the morning light and breathe deeply, absorbing the sun's warmth and energy. Let it fill you with vigor for the day ahead.

Affirmation: With every sunrise, I am recharged and invigorated, ready to face my day with confidence and energy.

Thought: The sun's rise reminds us that every day holds new energy and opportunities.

Focus: Energy and vitality from the natural world.

SACRED WISDOM – NATIVE ANERICAN MEDITATIONS, AFFIRMATIONS, AND REFLECTIONS

January 4

Meditation: Visualize the vast expanse of the plains, the endless horizon that stretches before you. Feel the openness invite limitless possibilities.

Affirmation: I embrace the vastness of possibilities. My potential is as limitless as the horizon.

Thought: The plains teach us about space and potential; in vastness, there is room to grow.

Focus: Limitless potential and personal growth.

January 5

Meditation: Think of the ancient mountains, their enduring strength and majesty. Draw upon their resilience and stand firm in your convictions.

Affirmation: I am steadfast and resolute, like the mountains. My resolve is unshakeable.

Thought: Mountains remind us of our strength to endure and the majesty of nature's creations.

Focus: Strength and steadfastness.

January 6

Meditation: Reflect on the wisdom of the elders, their words like gentle but firm guidance. Let their lessons soothe and guide you.

Affirmation: I carry the wisdom of the elders with me. Their teachings guide my steps and decisions.

Thought: Elders bridge our past and present, offering wisdom that guides future generations.

Focus: Learning from ancestral wisdom.

January 7

Meditation: Observe the stars in the night sky, each one a distant guardian. Feel connected to the vast universe, and to the countless generations who have gazed upon the same stars.

Affirmation: I am connected to the universe, guided by the stars and the spirits of my ancestors.

Thought: The stars remind us of our small place in the cosmos and the interconnectedness of all things.

Focus: Connection to the cosmos and ancestral guidance.

SACRED WISDOM – NATIVE ANERICAN MEDITATIONS, AFFIRMATIONS, AND REFLECTIONS

January 8

Meditation: Imagine the gentle rustle of leaves in a serene forest, a soft symphony that calms the mind. Let the peace of nature's quietude envelop you.

Affirmation: I am at peace in nature's embrace, finding serenity in its subtle sounds and sights.

Thought: The forest teaches us the beauty of quiet moments, showing us how peace can be found in stillness.

Focus: Finding peace in nature's quiet.

January 9

Meditation: Reflect on the journey of the caterpillar to butterfly, a symbol of transformation. Embrace the changes within yourself as natural and beautiful.

Affirmation: I am in a state of transformation, and each change brings me closer to realizing my true potential.

Thought: Transformation is a natural progression, just as the caterpillar becomes a butterfly, we too evolve.

Focus: Personal transformation and growth.

January 10

Meditation: Feel the crispness of the morning air as you step outside, refreshing and invigorating your spirit. Let this freshness clear your mind.

Affirmation: Each breath of fresh air rejuvenates my body and mind, offering clarity and refreshment.

Thought: The morning air is a daily renewal, a natural tonic for clarity and vigor.

Focus: Refreshment and clarity from nature.

SACRED WISDOM – NATIVE ANERICAN MEDITATIONS, AFFIRMATIONS, AND REFLECTIONS

January 11

Meditation: Visualize the warmth of a campfire on a chilly evening. Its glow represents community and warmth shared among friends and family.

Affirmation: I nurture and cherish the warmth of community, fostering connections that sustain and uplift me.

Thought: Just as a fire draws us together, so does the warmth of community strengthen our bonds.

Focus: The warmth and strength of community.

January 12

Meditation: Consider the enduring patience of the desert, where life flourishes despite harsh conditions. Emulate its resilience in your own life.

Affirmation: I embody resilience and patience, thriving in all circumstances, just as life persists in the desert.

Thought: The desert teaches us about resilience, showing how life adapts and thrives in adversity.

Focus: Resilience and adaptation.

January 13

Meditation: Listen to the rain's rhythmic pattering on the roof, a soothing, cleansing sound that washes away worries.

Affirmation: Each drop of rain cleanses my spirit, washing away concerns and replenishing my soul.

Thought: Rain is nature's cleanse, refreshing the earth and our spirits alike.

Focus: Cleansing and renewal.

SACRED WISDOM – NATIVE ANERICAN MEDITATIONS, AFFIRMATIONS, AND REFLECTIONS

January 14

Meditation: Observe the grandeur of an eagle soaring high above, a symbol of freedom and perspective. Seek to adopt its broad view on life's challenges.

Affirmation: I soar above life's challenges, embracing freedom and gaining perspective from my lofty view.

Thought: The eagle's flight teaches us about freedom and the importance of a higher perspective.

Focus: Freedom and perspective.

January 15

Meditation: Imagine walking along a mountain stream, the water clear and the path lined with stones. Feel the steadiness of the earth under your feet, grounding you.

Affirmation: I am grounded and steady, like the mountain path, secure in my journey through life.

Thought: The mountain stream, with its clear water and firm path, teaches us the importance of being grounded in our own lives.

Focus: Grounding and stability.

January 16

Meditation: Think of the quiet wisdom of the owl in the night. Embrace the depth of knowledge that comes with quiet observation and listening.

Affirmation: I seek wisdom in silence, learning much as I observe and listen attentively.

Thought: The owl's silent vigil reminds us that wisdom often comes not from speaking, but from listening and observing.

Focus: Wisdom through silence and observation.

SACRED WISDOM – NATIVE AMERICAN MEDITATIONS, AFFIRMATIONS, AND REFLECTIONS

January 17

Meditation: Feel the energy of a thunderstorm, its power and intensity a reminder of the forces that shape our world.

Affirmation: I harness the energy and power of the natural world, channeling it into positive action in my life.

Thought: Thunderstorms remind us of the raw power of nature, urging us to respect and harness such forces in our lives.

Focus: Channeling natural energy.

January 18

Meditation: Reflect on the pattern of the stars in the night sky, their constellations telling stories of old. Let these tales inspire a sense of continuity and connection.

Affirmation: I am connected to the ancient stories and wisdom of the stars, guided by their enduring light.

Thought: The stars not only illuminate our nights but also connect us to the ancient wisdom passed down through generations.

Focus: Connection to ancient wisdom.

January 19

Meditation: Contemplate the resilience of winter grass, enduring cold and snow yet still standing tall and green beneath.

Affirmation: I have the resilience of the winter grass, enduring challenges yet remaining vibrant and strong.

Thought: Winter grass, with its unyielding green vitality amid the cold, teaches us resilience and persistence.

Focus: Resilience and vitality.

SACRED WISDOM – NATIVE ANERICAN MEDITATIONS, AFFIRMATIONS, AND REFLECTIONS

January 20

Meditation: Imagine the calming sound of raindrops on a calm lake, each ripple spreading wide and blending back into the whole.

Affirmation: Like the lake touched by rain, I remain calm and adaptable, allowing life's moments to ripple through me without disturbance.

Thought: The lake's response to rain—a gentle ripple—teaches us to accept life's disturbances with calm and grace.

Focus: Calmness and adaptability.

January 21

Meditation: Consider the ancient practice of planting by the moon phases, a rhythm that ties agricultural success to celestial patterns.

Affirmation: I align my actions with the natural rhythms of the earth and sky, finding success in harmony with nature.

Thought: Planting by the moon phases reminds us of the wisdom in synchronizing our activities with the natural world's rhythms.

Focus: Harmony with natural rhythms.

January 22

Meditation: Picture the slow, majestic rise of the sun over a calm sea, its rays spreading warmth and light. Feel this warmth as a gentle, embracing energy.

Affirmation: Each sunrise fills me with warmth and hope, renewing my spirit for the day ahead.

Thought: The sunrise over the sea reminds us of new beginnings and the constant renewal of nature.

Focus: Renewal and hope.

SACRED WISDOM – NATIVE ANERICAN MEDITATIONS, AFFIRMATIONS, AND REFLECTIONS

January 23

Meditation: Envision the intricate weave of a spider's web, strong yet delicate. Appreciate the balance of resilience and subtlety in nature.

Affirmation: I balance strength and delicacy in my life, constructing my days with careful thought and resilience.

Thought: The spider's web, a marvel of natural engineering, teaches us the importance of balance in our lives.

Focus: Balance and careful construction.

January 24

Meditation: Reflect on the peaceful solitude of a winter's night, the world hushed and the air crisp. Embrace the quiet and allow it to soothe your thoughts.

Affirmation: I find peace in solitude, allowing the quiet of the night to bring clarity and calm to my mind.

Thought: A winter's night, with its serene silence, offers us a chance to pause and find peace within ourselves.

Focus: Solitude and peace.

January 25

Meditation: Imagine the end of a storm, the clouds parting to reveal a clear, fresh sky. Recognize this moment as a metaphor for overcoming challenges.

Affirmation: After every storm in my life, I emerge stronger and clearer, ready to face the world anew.

Thought: The clearing skies after a storm remind us that challenges are temporary and renewal is always possible.

Focus: Overcoming challenges and renewal.

SACRED WISDOM – NATIVE ANERICAN MEDITATIONS, AFFIRMATIONS, AND REFLECTIONS

January 26

Meditation: Think of the enduring strength of a rock sculpted by wind and water over millennia. Draw inspiration from its persistent shaping.

Affirmation: Like the rock shaped by elements, I am resilient and shaped by my experiences, growing ever stronger.

Thought: The sculpted rock shows us that time and persistence lead to beauty and strength, shaped by the environment.

Focus: Strength and resilience through time.

January 27

Meditation: Consider the cycle of the seasons, each bringing its own gifts and challenges. Recognize the beauty and necessity of each phase.

Affirmation: I embrace each season of my life, knowing that like nature, every phase has its unique beauty and purpose.

Thought: Just as the seasons cycle through the year, so do phases in our lives, each essential and enriching.

Focus: Embracing life's seasons.

January 28

Meditation: Visualize a field of wildflowers, each bloom a burst of color and life. Feel the joy and freedom these wild spaces evoke.

Affirmation: I embrace the wildness and diversity of life, finding joy and freedom in its vibrant expressions.

Thought: Wildflowers teach us about diversity and the spontaneous joy of nature, encouraging us to find beauty in life's variety.

Focus: Diversity and joy.

SACRED WISDOM – NATIVE ANERICAN MEDITATIONS, AFFIRMATIONS, AND REFLECTIONS

January 29

Meditation: Picture the slow ascent of fog on a mountainous landscape, enveloping everything in a gentle, mysterious embrace. Let its tranquility permeate your soul.

Affirmation: I am enveloped in the gentle mystery of life, moving through each day with a calm and centered spirit.

Thought: The fog on a mountain teaches us the beauty of mystery and the peace that comes with embracing the unknown.

Focus: Embracing mystery and tranquility.

January 30

Meditation: Feel the heartbeat of the earth through the rhythmic drumming at a gathering, connecting you to the pulse of life itself.

Affirmation: I am deeply connected to the rhythm of life, moving in harmony with the earth's deep and ancient heartbeat.

Thought: Drumming connects us not only to each other but to the very rhythm of the earth, reminding us of our shared pulse.

Focus: Connection and harmony with life's rhythms.

January 31

Meditation: Observe the gentle sway of trees in the wind, a dance of flexibility and strength. Let their movement inspire ease and resilience in your life.

Affirmation: Like the trees, I sway with the wind but remain rooted, embodying flexibility and strength in my life's challenges.

Thought: The swaying trees teach us to bend but not break, combining flexibility with enduring strength.

Focus: Flexibility and rooted strength.

SACRED WISDOM – NATIVE ANERICAN MEDITATIONS, AFFIRMATIONS, AND REFLECTIONS

February 1

Meditation: Imagine the first thaw of spring, the sound of ice melting and streams flowing freely again. Feel the release and renewal this brings.

Affirmation: As the ice melts, so do any barriers within me, allowing my spirit to flow freely and vibrantly.

Thought: The thaw signifies renewal and the refreshing flow of new beginnings, reminding us of nature's cycles of rebirth.

Focus: Renewal and flowing freely.

February 2

Meditation: Contemplate the enduring presence of mountains under the moonlight, their silhouettes a testament to resilience. Let their unyielding nature inspire you.

Affirmation: I am as resilient as the mountains under moonlight, standing strong through the passage of time.

Thought: Mountains remind us of our ability to endure, their steadfastness an inspiration across ages.

Focus: Steadfastness and enduring strength.

February 3

Meditation: Picture a lone wolf moving silently through the forest, its presence both powerful and elusive. Draw strength from its solitary but purposeful journey.

Affirmation: I move through life with the purpose and grace of the wolf, confident in my path and connected to my instincts.

Thought: The wolf's journey teaches us the power of purpose and the strength found in following our own instincts.

Focus: Purposefulness and instinctual guidance.

SACRED WISDOM – NATIVE ANERICAN MEDITATIONS, AFFIRMATIONS, AND REFLECTIONS

February 4

Meditation: Imagine the intricate patterns of frost on a windowpane, each unique and fleeting. Appreciate the beauty of temporary forms.

Affirmation: I see the beauty in fleeting moments, cherishing each one for its unique and temporary nature.

Thought: Frost patterns remind us that beauty can be transient, encouraging us to appreciate the present moment.

Focus: Appreciation of the moment and transient beauty.

February 5

Meditation: Visualize a quiet lake at dawn, the surface mirror-like and undisturbed. Feel the peace and stillness as a deep, calming influence.

Affirmation: I am as serene as a still lake, my mind clear and my spirit peaceful.

Thought: The stillness of a lake at dawn teaches us the value of calmness and the clarity it brings to our lives.

Focus: Serenity and clarity.

February 6

Meditation: Consider the vast expanse of the night sky, filled with stars that have lighted paths for generations. Let their enduring glow guide your way.

Affirmation: I am guided by the ancient light of the stars, finding direction and inspiration in their age-old paths.

Thought: The stars are not just points of light but guides, their histories interwoven with our own journeys.

Focus: Guidance and inspiration from the past.

SACRED WISDOM – NATIVE ANERICAN MEDITATIONS, AFFIRMATIONS, AND REFLECTIONS

February 7

Meditation: Reflect on the resilience of a seedling breaking through tough soil to reach the sunlight. Embrace the persistence and determination it embodies.

Affirmation: I have the persistence of a seedling, pushing through barriers to grow and thrive in the light of my achievements.

Thought: The journey of a seedling is a powerful metaphor for personal growth, overcoming challenges to reach new heights.

Focus: Persistence and personal growth.

February 8

Meditation: Imagine the soft whisper of the wind through tall prairie grass, a soothing sound that speaks of resilience and adaptation.

Affirmation: I adapt with grace, bending like the prairie grass when challenges arise, yet always standing tall again.

Thought: Prairie grass, bending yet unbroken by the wind, teaches us the beauty of resilience and the strength in flexibility.

Focus: Adaptation and resilience.

February 9

Meditation: Feel the warmth of a fire during a cold night, its flames dancing lively and providing comfort and light. Let this warmth fill your heart.

Affirmation: I carry the warmth of kindness within me, spreading light and comfort to those around me.

Thought: The fire's warmth on a cold night reminds us of the importance of providing light and warmth to others in their times of need.

Focus: Kindness and providing comfort.

SACRED WISDOM – NATIVE ANERICAN MEDITATIONS, AFFIRMATIONS, AND REFLECTIONS

February 10

Meditation: Picture the slow, graceful flow of a river carving its path through the land. Let its persistent, gentle force inspire your own journey.

Affirmation: I flow through life with grace and determination, carving my path just as the river shapes the land.

Thought: The river, with its graceful and determined flow, teaches us the power of gentle persistence over time.

Focus: Graceful determination.

February 11

Meditation: Observe the harmony of a forest ecosystem, each element from the soil to the canopy interdependent and thriving. Draw inspiration from this natural balance.

Affirmation: I live in harmony with my surroundings, contributing to and drawing from the communal balance.

Thought: The forest exemplifies perfect balance and interdependence, a model for us to strive toward in our own communities.

Focus: Harmony and balance in life.

February 12

Meditation: Imagine the first light of dawn piercing through the darkness, symbolizing hope and new opportunities. Let this light renew your spirit.

Affirmation: With each new dawn, I embrace fresh opportunities and the hope they bring, renewing my spirit each day.

Thought: The dawn's first light breaks the night's darkness, reminding us that every day holds new potential and beginnings.

Focus: Renewal and hope with each new day.

SACRED WISDOM – NATIVE ANERICAN MEDITATIONS, AFFIRMATIONS, AND REFLECTIONS

February 13

Meditation: Picture the gentle touch of snowflakes falling silently, each one unique and perfect. Feel the quiet beauty of their unassuming presence.

Affirmation: I recognize and celebrate my unique beauty and the quiet contributions I make to the world.

Thought: Snowflakes, each distinct and delicate, remind us of the value of our individual uniqueness in the tapestry of life.

Focus: Celebrating uniqueness and quiet contributions.

February 14

Meditation: Feel the embrace of the earth as you walk barefoot on the grass, connecting with its energy and stability.

Affirmation: I am grounded and supported by the earth, drawing strength and stability from its enduring presence.

Thought: Walking barefoot on the earth reconnects us to its natural energy, reminding us of our roots and the support it offers.

Focus: Grounding and drawing strength from the earth.

February 15

Meditation: Reflect on the lifecycle of a leaf, from its budding in spring to its colorful death in autumn. Each phase holds beauty and purpose.

Affirmation: I accept and find beauty in each phase of my life, knowing that every stage has its purpose and grace.

Thought: Just like the leaf, our lives cycle through phases of growth and change, each important and beautiful in its way.

Focus: Acceptance and beauty in life's phases.

SACRED WISDOM – NATIVE AMERICAN MEDITATIONS, AFFIRMATIONS, AND REFLECTIONS

February 16

Meditation: Consider the calm that descends with a heavy snowfall, the world quiet and insulated. Let this peace envelop your mind.

Affirmation: I find peace in stillness, allowing myself moments of quiet solitude to refresh my spirit.

Thought: A snow-covered landscape teaches us the peace that can be found in stillness, a quiet world where we can reflect and rejuvenate.

Focus: Peace in stillness and reflection.

February 17

Meditation: Visualize a hawk soaring high above the earth, its keen eyes sharp and focused. Draw inspiration from its clarity and high perspective.

Affirmation: I maintain a clear and focused perspective on my goals, soaring above distractions like the hawk above the earth.

Thought: The hawk's flight reminds us of the benefits of viewing things from a higher perspective, focusing on what truly matters.

Focus: Clarity and perspective in life's journey.

February 18

Meditation: Imagine the rhythmic pounding of a waterfall, its powerful flow relentless and inspiring. Feel the energy and power it represents.

Affirmation: I embrace the relentless energy and power within me, using it to overcome obstacles and flow forward with strength.

Thought: Waterfalls, with their powerful and continuous flow, teach us about the relentless strength within that drives us forward.

Focus: Inner strength and relentless progress.

SACRED WISDOM – NATIVE ANERICAN MEDITATIONS, AFFIRMATIONS, AND REFLECTIONS

February 19

Meditation: Consider the intricate dance of flames within a fire, each one independent yet part of a collective energy. Embrace the balance between individuality and unity.

Affirmation: I am both a unique individual and a vital part of my community, blending my personal energy with others to create something greater.

Thought: A fire's collective flames remind us that while each of us is distinct, together we create a powerful and cohesive energy.

Focus: Balancing individuality with community.

February 20

Meditation: Picture the enduring presence of an ancient tree, its roots deep and branches high. Draw strength from its longevity and resilience.

Affirmation: I am rooted in my past and reaching towards my future, drawing strength from my history and growing ever upward.

Thought: Ancient trees remind us of the strength that comes from deep roots and the growth that reaches new heights.

Focus: Strength from roots and growth towards the future.

February 21

Meditation: Reflect on the serene beauty of a butterfly garden, each creature a delicate artwork of nature. Embrace the peacefulness and diversity around you.

Affirmation: I appreciate and thrive in the diversity of life, finding beauty and peace in the variety of the world's expressions.

Thought: A butterfly garden's diversity teaches us about the beauty of individuality and the harmony of different beings coexisting.

Focus: Appreciating diversity and finding peace in harmony.

SACRED WISDOM – NATIVE AMERICAN MEDITATIONS, AFFIRMATIONS, AND REFLECTIONS

February 22

Meditation: Imagine the soft murmur of a brook as it travels over pebbles and through the woods. Let its continuous, gentle sound soothe your spirit.

Affirmation: I flow through life's challenges with ease, like a brook smoothly navigating around obstacles, always moving forward.

Thought: The brook's journey is a lesson in persistence and adaptability, showing how to move gracefully through life's terrain.

Focus: Graceful navigation through life's challenges.

February 23

Meditation: Visualize the stark beauty of a desert at sunset, the colors vivid against the sparse landscape. Find beauty in simplicity and vastness.

Affirmation: I find profound beauty in simplicity, recognizing that there is vastness and depth in unadorned truth.

Thought: The desert at sunset teaches us that there is striking beauty in simplicity and strength in the sparsest conditions.

Focus: Beauty in simplicity and finding strength in minimalism.

February 24

Meditation: Feel the energy of a stormy sea, its waves powerful and commanding. Harness this dynamic energy to fuel your own endeavors.

Affirmation: I channel the dynamic energy of the sea, using its powerful force to propel my actions and achieve my goals.

Thought: The stormy sea, with its untamed energy, reminds us of the powerful forces within us waiting to be harnessed.

Focus: Harnessing internal energy for powerful actions.

SACRED WISDOM – NATIVE ANERICAN MEDITATIONS, AFFIRMATIONS, AND REFLECTIONS

February 25

Meditation: Observe the quiet majesty of a snow-capped mountain, serene and imposing. Let its enduring presence inspire a sense of peace and steadfastness.

Affirmation: I am as serene and steadfast as a mountain, unshaken by the chaos around me, maintaining my inner peace.

Thought: Snow-capped mountains, standing firm against the elements, teach us about the power of serenity and the strength of steadfastness.

Focus: Serenity and steadfastness in life's challenges.

February 26

Meditation: Imagine the resilience of a cliff face, standing against the winds and waves of time. Embrace its unyielding strength and enduring nature.

Affirmation: I am resilient and enduring, like the cliff face against the sea, standing strong through the tests of time and challenge.

Thought: The cliff, exposed yet unyielding, teaches us about the resilience required to face life's relentless challenges.

Focus: Endurance and resilience against life's trials.

February 27

Meditation: Reflect on the gentle unfolding of a fern frond, a natural example of elegance and grace in growth. Let this natural progression inspire your own development.

Affirmation: I grow with grace and elegance, unfolding my potential gently and steadily, like the fern in the forest.

Thought: The fern's growth, slow and elegant, reminds us that our own development can be a graceful and natural progression.

Focus: Graceful growth and natural development.

SACRED WISDOM – NATIVE ANERICAN MEDITATIONS, AFFIRMATIONS, AND REFLECTIONS

February 28

Meditation: Visualize the silent majesty of a snowy owl in flight, its wings spread wide against the twilight sky. Embrace the quiet confidence and focus it embodies.

Affirmation: I move through life with quiet confidence and focus, my path as clear and purposeful as the owl's flight through the night.

Thought: The snowy owl's silent flight teaches us the power of moving with purpose and confidence, undistracted by the noise around us.

Focus: Quiet confidence and purposeful action.

March 1

Meditation: Consider the deep, rhythmic sound of a drumbeat echoing in the night, connecting those who hear it across time and space. Feel this connection deep in your soul.

Affirmation: I am connected to the rhythm of life, my heart beating in sync with those around me, creating a symphony of shared experiences.

Thought: The drumbeat, a universal sound, connects us not just to each other but to our ancestors and the earth itself.

Focus: Connection through shared rhythms.

March 2

Meditation: Picture the early morning mist hovering over a calm river, the world around it awakening slowly. Let the peace of this slow awakening settle in you.

Affirmation: I embrace the peace of a slow awakening, finding clarity and calm in the gentle start of each new day.

Thought: The morning mist over a river reminds us of the value of waking slowly, the peace of gradual beginnings offering clarity.

Focus: Peaceful and slow awakenings.

SACRED WISDOM – NATIVE ANERICAN MEDITATIONS, AFFIRMATIONS, AND REFLECTIONS

March 3

Meditation: Reflect on the vibrant life within a coral reef, a bustling ecosystem full of color and life. Draw inspiration from its diversity and vibrancy.

Affirmation: I thrive in diversity, my life enriched by the various colors and forms that surround me, much like a vibrant coral reef.

Thought: The coral reef, with its complex and colorful ecosystem, teaches us the beauty and strength of diversity.

Focus: Embracing and thriving in diversity.

March 4

Meditation: Feel the solid ground under a towering redwood tree, its roots deep and wide. Draw strength from its connection to the earth and longevity.

Affirmation: I am deeply rooted and connected, drawing strength and stability from my foundations, as steadfast as the redwood.

Thought: Redwoods, with their profound roots and impressive heights, teach us the importance of a strong foundation for enduring success.

Focus: Strength and stability from deep roots.

March 5

Meditation: Envision the powerful surge of a river after a rainstorm, its waters swollen and vigorous. Let this force remind you of your own inner strength and vitality.

Affirmation: I possess a powerful inner strength, surging within me like a river, capable of overcoming any obstacle in my path.

Thought: The vitality of a swollen river teaches us about the powerful forces within us, ready to be harnessed to forge our path forward.

Focus: Harnessing inner strength and vitality.

SACRED WISDOM – NATIVE ANERICAN MEDITATIONS, AFFIRMATIONS, AND REFLECTIONS

March 6

Meditation: Contemplate the vast silence of a desert under the moonlight, its stillness profound and enveloping. Embrace this deep quietude within yourself.

Affirmation: I find profound stillness within, a quietude as deep as the desert night, bringing clarity and peace to my soul.

Thought: The silent expanse of the desert at night teaches us the value of embracing stillness, finding peace in quiet reflection.

Focus: Embracing stillness and inner peace.

March 7

Meditation: Picture the first buds of spring pushing through the snow, symbols of persistence and renewal. Let their resilience inspire your own rebirth.

Affirmation: I am resilient and ready for renewal, like the spring buds pushing through the last snow, signaling new beginnings and growth.

Thought: The emergence of spring buds through snow reminds us of the unstoppable force of life and renewal, urging us to embrace new growth.

Focus: Renewal and embracing new beginnings.

March 8

Meditation: Reflect on the calm and steady gaze of a deer in the forest, alert yet at peace in its environment. Seek to emulate its balanced state of awareness and calm.

Affirmation: I maintain a calm awareness in my surroundings, poised and peaceful like a deer in the forest, attuned to my environment.

Thought: The deer's tranquil presence in the forest teaches us the importance of being both aware and at peace in our own lives.

Focus: Balanced awareness and tranquility.

SACRED WISDOM – NATIVE ANERICAN MEDITATIONS, AFFIRMATIONS, AND REFLECTIONS

March 9

Meditation: Visualize a clear sky at twilight, the transition of colors a painting of nature's own making. Let the sky's vastness inspire your dreams.

Affirmation: I am inspired by the limitless sky, my dreams as vast and varied as the hues of twilight, open to endless possibilities.

Thought: The ever-changing sky at twilight reminds us that transitions are beautiful and filled with potential, inspiring us to dream without limits.

Focus: Inspiration and limitless possibilities.

March 10

Meditation: Think of the gentle folding of hills in a landscape, their undulations soft and rhythmic. Let their rolling continuity soothe your spirit.

Affirmation: I find rhythm and comfort in life's gentle undulations, moving through its highs and lows with graceful continuity.

Thought: The rolling hills teach us about the gentle, rhythmic nature of life's journey, encouraging us to embrace its ups and downs with grace.

Focus: Embracing life's rhythm and continuity.

March 11

Meditation: Feel the warmth of the sun on your face during a brisk early spring day, its light more welcome as it breaks through the chill air. Embrace the warmth as a source of renewal and energy.

Affirmation: I embrace the renewing energy of the sun, letting its warmth energize and revitalize my spirit, breaking through the last of winter's chill.

Thought: The sun's warmth on a cold spring day reminds us of the power of light and warmth to renew and energize, signaling the end of the cold and the beginning of growth.

Focus: Renewal and energizing warmth.

SACRED WISDOM – NATIVE ANERICAN MEDITATIONS, AFFIRMATIONS, AND REFLECTIONS

March 12

Meditation: Imagine the silent vigil of the night sky, stars scattered like ancient guides. Let the timeless watch of these celestial bodies inspire a sense of continuity and connection.

Affirmation: I am guided by the ancient stars, connected to the timeless wisdom they hold, feeling part of a continuous cosmic journey.

Thought: The night sky, with its silent stars, connects us to past generations who navigated their lives by these same lights, reminding us of our place in a larger story.

Focus: Connection to ancient wisdom and continuity.

March 13

Meditation: Consider the soft whisper of falling leaves, each descent a gentle journey towards the earth. Let this quiet and steady release inspire your own releases in life.

Affirmation: I release what no longer serves me with the grace of a falling leaf, gently and without fear, making room for new growth.

Thought: The falling leaves teach us about the natural cycle of release and renewal, a necessary process for new beginnings and growth.

Focus: Graceful release and renewal.

March 14

Meditation: Picture the steadfastness of a boulder amidst a rushing stream, water flowing around it. Emulate its unwavering presence in the face of constant change.

Affirmation: I am steadfast and unyielding in my core values, like a boulder in a stream, regardless of the changes around me.

Thought: The boulder in the stream teaches us resilience and steadfastness, standing firm despite the relentless flow of life around it.

Focus: Steadfastness and resilience amidst change.

March 15

Meditation: Feel the life-giving force of rain nourishing the parched earth, each drop a promise of growth and renewal. Let this nurturing act inspire your own efforts to support and renew.

Affirmation: I nourish and renew myself and others, bringing life and growth wherever I go, like rain to parched earth.

Thought: Rain's nurturing touch on the earth reminds us of the importance of care and renewal, both for ourselves and our communities.

Focus: Nurturing and supporting growth.

March 16

Meditation: Envision the expansive view from a mountain peak, the world stretched out below. Let the broad perspective inspire a greater understanding and vision in your life.

Affirmation: From this high vantage point, I gain clarity and a broader understanding of my life's path, inspired by the expansive view before me.

Thought: The view from a mountain peak teaches us to look beyond immediate circumstances and embrace a wider perspective on our lives.

Focus: Gaining perspective and understanding.

March 17

Meditation: Reflect on the rhythmic pattern of a bird in flight, each wingbeat perfectly timed and efficient. Let this natural rhythm and efficiency inspire your actions.

Affirmation: I move through life with the efficiency and rhythm of a bird in flight, each action purposeful and well-timed.

Thought: The bird's flight, with its rhythmic and efficient movements, teaches us the importance of timing and grace in our own actions.

Focus: Efficiency and rhythmic timing in actions.

SACRED WISDOM – NATIVE ANERICAN MEDITATIONS, AFFIRMATIONS, AND REFLECTIONS

March 18

Meditation: Observe the quiet resilience of wildlife during a winter snow, their survival a testament to adaptability and strength. Draw inspiration from their endurance.

Affirmation: I embody the resilience and adaptability of wildlife in winter, enduring challenges with strength and grace.

Thought: The resilience of animals in winter reminds us of our own capacity to adapt and endure, even under difficult conditions.

Focus: Resilience and adaptability in adversity.

March 19

Meditation: Imagine the soothing rhythm of ocean waves lapping gently at the shore, a calming, repetitive sound that washes away worries.

Affirmation: I allow the rhythm of the ocean to calm my mind, washing away worries and bringing peace to my soul.

Thought: The ocean's gentle waves remind us of the soothing power of nature's rhythms, offering peace and renewal with each wave.

Focus: Calming rhythms and mental renewal.

March 20

Meditation: Picture the first green shoots of grass emerging from the frost, a vibrant sign of life renewing itself. Let this vigor and resilience inspire your own rebirth.

Affirmation: I embrace the resilience and vigor of new growth, renewing myself with fresh energy and perspectives.

Thought: The emergence of green grass after the cold shows us the unstoppable nature of renewal and growth, urging us to rejuvenate our spirits.

Focus: Renewal and embracing new growth.

SACRED WISDOM – NATIVE ANERICAN MEDITATIONS, AFFIRMATIONS, AND REFLECTIONS

March 21

Meditation: Reflect on the majestic flight of a flock of birds across the sunset, their coordinated movements a dance of unity and grace.

Affirmation: I move in harmony with those around me, finding strength and beauty in our shared journeys and collective goals.

Thought: The flight of birds, especially at sunset, teaches us about the beauty and strength found in unity and coordinated effort.

Focus: Unity and coordinated movements.

March 22

Meditation: Consider the enduring solidity of a granite rock, shaped and smoothed over millennia. Draw strength from its unyielding nature and historical endurance.

Affirmation: I am as solid and enduring as granite, withstanding the test of time and emerging smoother and stronger.

Thought: Granite, with its solid and enduring presence, teaches us the virtues of strength, resilience, and the beauty of being shaped by time.

Focus: Endurance and resilience through time.

March 23

Meditation: Envision the vast canopy of a forest, each tree connected and interdependent. Let this ecosystem inspire your sense of community and interconnectedness.

Affirmation: I am an integral part of my community, connected and contributing to the strength and health of the whole, like a tree in a vast forest.

Thought: The forest canopy, with its interdependent network, teaches us the importance of community and the strength found in connections.

Focus: Community strength and interconnectedness.

March 24

Meditation: Feel the warmth of early spring sunlight breaking through bare branches, its light promising warmth and renewal. Let this promise invigorate your spirit.

Affirmation: I am rejuvenated by the promise of renewal, feeling the warmth of new possibilities energize my soul.

Thought: The early spring sun, breaking through the cold, reminds us that warmth and renewal are always just moments away.

Focus: Promise of renewal and invigoration.

March 25

Meditation: Picture the slow, dignified ascent of a hot air balloon at dawn, rising quietly over a tranquil landscape. Embrace the peaceful ascent and broadening view.

Affirmation: I rise above life's challenges with dignity and peace, gaining a broader perspective with each experience.

Thought: The ascent of a hot air balloon at dawn teaches us the value of rising above the fray, embracing peace and gaining perspective as we ascend.

Focus: Peaceful ascent and broadening perspectives.

March 26

Meditation: Visualize the steadfast presence of an ancient oak tree, its branches widespread, offering shelter and strength. Embrace its enduring stability and protective nature.

Affirmation: I am as strong and sheltering as an ancient oak, providing strength and protection to those around me, rooted deeply in my own stability.

Thought: The ancient oak, with its protective branches and deep roots, teaches us about strength, stability, and the importance of offering shelter to others.

Focus: Strength, stability, and protection.

SACRED WISDOM – NATIVE AMERICAN MEDITATIONS, AFFIRMATIONS, AND REFLECTIONS

March 27

Meditation: Imagine the delicate balance of a dewdrop poised on a leaf tip at dawn, a perfect sphere reflecting the new light. Let this balance inspire poise and clarity in your life.

Affirmation: I maintain balance and poise in my life, reflecting clarity and light in my actions and thoughts, like a dewdrop in the morning sun.

Thought: The dewdrop's precarious yet perfect balance teaches us the beauty of maintaining composure and clarity amidst life's delicate situations.

Focus: Balance, poise, and clarity.

March 28

Meditation: Contemplate the quiet power of a glacier, slowly shaping the landscape beneath it, unstoppable in its gradual movement. Draw strength from its persistent force.

Affirmation: I embody the quiet, unstoppable force of a glacier, shaping my future with persistent, powerful movements.

Thought: Glaciers, with their slow yet powerful force, remind us that profound changes often come gradually, shaped by steady persistence.

Focus: Quiet power and persistent change.

March 29

Meditation: Reflect on the harmonious chorus of a dawn chorus, birds of different species singing together. Let this symphony of sounds encourage unity and cooperation in your life.

Affirmation: I live in harmony with those around me, contributing to and cherishing our shared symphony of existence, like birds in a dawn chorus.

Thought: The dawn chorus, with its varied yet harmonious melodies, teaches us the beauty of diverse voices coming together in cooperation.

Focus: Harmony, unity, and cooperation.

SACRED WISDOM – NATIVE ANERICAN MEDITATIONS, AFFIRMATIONS, AND REFLECTIONS

March 30

Meditation: Picture the ebb and flow of the tides, governed by the moon's pull. This natural rhythm, constant and reassuring, inspires you to embrace life's phases with grace.

Affirmation: I embrace the ebb and flow of my life, confident in the natural rhythms that guide my days, finding reassurance in their constancy.

Thought: The tides, with their reliable patterns, teach us the value of accepting the natural cycles of life, each phase bringing its own gifts.

Focus: Embracing life's natural rhythms.

March 31

Meditation: Feel the gentle touch of spring rain on your face, each drop a promise of renewal and growth. Let this nurturing rainfall cleanse and refresh your spirit.

Affirmation: I welcome renewal with each drop of spring rain, feeling cleansed and rejuvenated, ready to grow and flourish anew.

Thought: Spring rain, gentle yet persistent, reminds us of the cleansing power of renewal, washing away the old to nourish the new.

Focus: Cleansing, renewal, and growth.

April 1

Meditation: Consider the playful dance of butterflies over a meadow, their movements light and carefree. Embrace this sense of lightness and joy in your own life.

Affirmation: I embody the lightness and joy of butterflies, my spirit dancing carefree through the meadows of my life, embracing each moment with delight.

Thought: Butterflies, with their carefree and joyful dance, teach us the importance of embracing lightness and finding joy in simple pleasures.

Focus: Lightness, joy, and embracing the moment.

SACRED WISDOM – NATIVE ANERICAN MEDITATIONS, AFFIRMATIONS, AND REFLECTIONS

April 2

Meditation: Imagine the first light of dawn breaking across a still lake, the surface perfectly reflecting the changing colors of the sky. Let this scene inspire a reflective and serene start to your day.

Affirmation: I reflect serenity and calm, like a still lake at dawn, starting each day with peace and clarity in my heart.

Thought: The calm lake at dawn teaches us about reflection and the peace that comes with a clear, tranquil mind.

Focus: Serenity, reflection, and a peaceful start.

April 3

Meditation: Picture the strength and grace of a river cutting through a canyon, its waters shaping the hard rock over centuries. Let this powerful persistence inspire your own path through life's challenges.

Affirmation: I am persistent and strong, carving my path through life with determination and grace, like a river shapes a canyon.

Thought: The river through the canyon reminds us that even the hardest obstacles can be shaped and overcome with persistent effort.

Focus: Persistence, strength, and overcoming challenges.

April 4

Meditation: Envision the intricate patterns of frost on a window, each design unique and delicate. Let the beauty of these fleeting artworks inspire appreciation for life's ephemeral moments.

Affirmation: I appreciate and cherish the fleeting, beautiful moments of life, recognizing their transient beauty like frost's delicate patterns.

Thought: The delicate frost patterns teach us about the beauty of transience, urging us to appreciate the moment before it fades.

Focus: Appreciation of transience and beauty.

SACRED WISDOM – NATIVE AMERICAN MEDITATIONS, AFFIRMATIONS, AND REFLECTIONS

April 5

Meditation: Contemplate the quiet endurance of a desert surviving the scorching day and embracing the cold night. Embrace this adaptability and resilience in your own life.

Affirmation: I adapt with resilience to life's extremes, enduring challenges with the quiet strength of a desert.

Thought: The desert's survival through extreme conditions teaches us about resilience and the power of adaptation in adverse environments.

Focus: Resilience, adaptation, and enduring strength.

April 6

Meditation: Consider the burst of energy in a forest awakening in the spring, every creature and plant bursting to life. Let this vigor and renewal energize your spirit.

Affirmation: I am energized by the renewal around me, embracing the vigor of spring to rejuvenate my spirit and body.

Thought: The vibrant awakening of a spring forest reminds us of the cyclic rejuvenation of life, inspiring us to embrace our own renewals.

Focus: Energy, renewal, and awakening.

April 7

Meditation: Watch the sunset painting the sky with colors so vibrant they seem to speak. Let the beauty of this daily closing inspire a grateful reflection on the day's gifts.

Affirmation: I reflect with gratitude on each day, embracing its end with the beauty and peace of a vibrant sunset.

Thought: The sunset, with its spectacular colors, teaches us to close each day with appreciation and peace, reflecting on the beauty it brought.

Focus: Gratitude and reflective closure.

SACRED WISDOM – NATIVE AMERICAN MEDITATIONS, AFFIRMATIONS, AND REFLECTIONS

April 8

Meditation: Feel the embrace of a foggy morning, its mist cloaking the world in mystery and softness. Let this gentle envelopment encourage you to find comfort in the unknown.

Affirmation: I find comfort in mystery and the unknown, embracing life's uncertainties with the soft courage of a foggy embrace.

Thought: A foggy morning softens our view, reminding us that not all must be clear to be navigated and that there is beauty in the unknown.

Focus: Comfort in mystery and embracing the unknown.

April 9

Meditation: Imagine the gentle touch of early morning dew on spring flowers, each droplet enhancing the flowers' vibrant colors. Let this image remind you of the rejuvenating power of nature.

Affirmation: I embrace nature's rejuvenating touch, allowing it to refresh and enhance my spirit, just as dew refreshes the morning flowers.

Thought: Morning dew on flowers not only nourishes but highlights their beauty, teaching us the value of gentle rejuvenation in our own lives.

Focus: Rejuvenation and natural beauty.

April 10

Meditation: Picture the enduring flight of geese migrating across vast distances, guided by instinct and the changing seasons. Let their determination and adaptability inspire your journey.

Affirmation: I am guided by my instincts and the rhythms of nature, finding direction and strength in my life's journey, like migrating geese.

Thought: The migration of geese is a testament to the power of instinct and the necessity of adaptation, guiding us through our own life changes.

Focus: Instinctual guidance and adaptation.

SACRED WISDOM – NATIVE ANERICAN MEDITATIONS, AFFIRMATIONS, AND REFLECTIONS

April 11

Meditation: Reflect on the silent majesty of towering redwoods, their presence a link between earth and sky. Draw strength from their ancient stability and continuous growth.

Affirmation: I draw strength from my roots and reach upward with ambition, like the redwoods, connecting my foundation with my aspirations.

Thought: Redwoods, reaching skyward for centuries, teach us about growth from strong foundations, inspiring us to grow tall and steadfast.

Focus: Growth from strong foundations.

April 12

Meditation: Feel the soothing rhythm of rain tapping on a rooftop during a gentle storm, each drop a heartbeat of nature. Let this rhythmic sound calm and center you.

Affirmation: I find rhythm and peace in life's simple moments, allowing the natural cadence of rain to bring tranquility to my mind and soul.

Thought: The rhythmic patter of rain not only nourishes the earth but soothes the spirit, offering a peaceful retreat from the chaos of daily life.

Focus: Finding peace in nature's rhythms.

April 13

Meditation: Consider the crisp clarity of a mountain view after a rain, the air fresh and the landscape vivid. Let this clear vision inspire clarity in your own thoughts and goals.

Affirmation: I embrace clarity and freshness in my outlook, inspired by the crisp view of mountains after rain, seeing my path and choices with renewed vision.

Thought: The clear view following a mountain rain teaches us the value of clarity and refreshment in our perspectives, clearing the way for precise vision.

Focus: Clarity of vision and freshness of perspective.

SACRED WISDOM – NATIVE AMERICAN MEDITATIONS, AFFIRMATIONS, AND REFLECTIONS

April 14

Meditation: Envision the slow, deliberate growth of a coral reef, each piece contributing to a vibrant ecosystem. Recognize the importance of each small contribution to the greater whole.

Affirmation: I acknowledge and value every small contribution I make, understanding that like a coral reef, every bit adds to a greater, vibrant whole.

Thought: Coral reefs grow slowly, each part crucial to the ecosystem's health, reminding us that small contributions are essential to larger successes.

Focus: Valuing small contributions.

April 15

Meditation: Watch the sun break through clouds after a storm, its light more appreciated for its absence. Let this renewal of light inspire optimism and hope in your life.

Affirmation: I welcome light and hope after challenges, just as the sun emerges brighter after a storm, reminding me of the renewal that follows hardships.

Thought: The sun's return after a storm is a powerful symbol of renewal and hope, encouraging us to remain optimistic through life's darker moments.

Focus: Optimism and renewal after challenges.

April 16

Meditation: Imagine the nurturing silence of a thick forest, where each tree stands as a guardian of tranquility. Let this forest envelop you in its peaceful embrace.

Affirmation: I am surrounded by peace, drawing calm and strength from the silent guardianship of the forest around me.

Thought: The forest's quiet is not merely absence of noise, but a rich, nurturing presence that teaches us how to find peace in solitude.

Focus: Embracing peace and solitude.

SACRED WISDOM – NATIVE ANERICAN MEDITATIONS, AFFIRMATIONS, AND REFLECTIONS

April 17

Meditation: Picture the cyclic journey of the moon, waxing and waning through phases. Each stage is essential, reflecting the beauty of change and renewal.

Affirmation: I embrace the cycles of my life with grace, recognizing the beauty and necessity of each phase, just as the moon gracefully transitions through its stages.

Thought: The moon's phases remind us that life is a series of cycles, each with its own beauty and purpose, essential to the whole.

Focus: Embracing life's cycles.

April 18

Meditation: Feel the exhilaration of a bird soaring high above, free from earthly constraints. Let this vision inspire a sense of freedom and possibility in your own life.

Affirmation: I soar in freedom and possibility, my spirit unbounded, embracing the vast opportunities that life offers.

Thought: The freedom of a bird in flight teaches us about potential and liberation, encouraging us to explore life beyond conventional boundaries.

Focus: Exploring freedom and potential.

April 19

Meditation: Consider the warm, golden glow of a sunset bathing the earth, its light soft and enveloping. Let this gentle end to the day bring you a sense of closure and readiness for renewal.

Affirmation: I welcome the end of each day with gratitude, allowing the soft glow of sunset to bring peaceful closure and prepare me for renewal.

Thought: Sunsets not only mark the end of day but also the beauty of endings and the promise of new beginnings, teaching us to appreciate the cycle of day and night.

Focus: Peaceful endings and new beginnings.

SACRED WISDOM – NATIVE AMERICAN MEDITATIONS, AFFIRMATIONS, AND REFLECTIONS

April 20

Meditation: Reflect on the intricate dance of fireflies at night, their lights flickering in darkness. Let their spontaneous light inspire joy and creativity in your life.

Affirmation: I embrace moments of spontaneous joy and creativity, inspired by the light and dance of fireflies, bringing brightness to the dark.

Thought: Fireflies illuminate the night with their fleeting light, showing us how spontaneous joy can light up the darkest times.

Focus: Joy and creativity in the moment.

April 21

Meditation: Envision the relentless power of a waterfall, its water cascading down with fierce beauty. Let the waterfall's energy and persistence inspire your endeavors.

Affirmation: I channel the waterfall's energy and persistence in my actions, approaching my goals with relentless vigor and determination.

Thought: The waterfall, with its powerful and incessant flow, teaches us the strength of persistence and the beauty of powerful endeavors.

Focus: Persistence and powerful actions.

April 22

Meditation: Imagine the quiet growth of a seed beneath the soil, unseen yet vital. Recognize the importance of what happens below the surface in your own growth and development.

Affirmation: I value the silent, inner work of my growth, knowing that like a seed's quiet growth under the soil, important changes are often unseen.

Thought: The unseen growth of a seed reminds us that essential developments in life and character often occur out of sight, laying foundations for future emergence.

Focus: Valuing inner growth and development.

SACRED WISDOM – NATIVE ANERICAN MEDITATIONS, AFFIRMATIONS, AND REFLECTIONS

April 23

Meditation: Consider the ancient rhythm of the ocean's tides, guided by the moon and unchanged by time. Let this eternal rhythm bring a sense of stability and continuity to your life.

Affirmation: I find stability and guidance in life's eternal rhythms, drawing peace from the unchanging dance of the ocean's tides.

Thought: The ocean tides, rhythmic and constant, remind us of the enduring patterns in nature that provide stability and continuity through time.

Focus: Stability and continuity in life's rhythms.

April 24

Meditation: Picture the first rays of sunlight filtering through a dense forest, illuminating paths hidden in darkness. Let this light guide you to find new ways forward in your own life.

Affirmation: I welcome the light that guides me through darkness, finding new paths and solutions as the forest light reveals hidden ways.

Thought: The light through the forest teaches us that even in darkness, there are paths waiting to be revealed, guiding us forward with newfound clarity.

Focus: Finding guidance and clarity.

April 25

Meditation: Reflect on the serene flow of a mountain stream, its waters clear and purposeful, overcoming obstacles with graceful ease. Embrace this fluid approach to life's challenges.

Affirmation: I navigate life's challenges with the grace and purpose of a mountain stream, flowing smoothly around obstacles in my path.

Thought: The mountain stream, with its clear and steady flow, teaches us the art of moving past obstacles with grace and resilience.

Focus: Graceful resilience in overcoming obstacles.

SACRED WISDOM – NATIVE ANERICAN MEDITATIONS, AFFIRMATIONS, AND REFLECTIONS

April 26

Meditation: Imagine the vibrant life within a blooming garden, each plant and flower contributing to a tapestry of colors and scents. Draw inspiration from this diversity and unity.

Affirmation: I thrive in diversity, each unique aspect of my life contributing to a beautiful, harmonious whole, like a garden in full bloom.

Thought: A blooming garden is a celebration of diversity and unity, showing us how varied elements can come together to create something beautiful and whole.

Focus: Celebrating diversity and unity.

April 27

Meditation: Consider the endurance of the hawk gliding high above the earth, utilizing currents to sustain its flight effortlessly. Let this efficient use of energy inspire your own efforts.

Affirmation: I use my energy efficiently, soaring through life's tasks with ease like a hawk riding the wind, maximizing my efforts with minimal strain.

Thought: The hawk's flight, sustained by air currents with minimal effort, teaches us to find and utilize the currents in our own lives for efficient and sustained effort.

Focus: Efficiency and ease in efforts.

April 28

Meditation: Feel the peace of a quiet snowfall, the world hushed and soft under a blanket of white. Let this quiet and gentle transformation inspire a peaceful renewal in your own life.

Affirmation: I embrace peaceful transformations, allowing a quiet renewal to unfold in my life, like the soft covering of a snowfall.

Thought: Snowfall transforms the landscape quietly but profoundly, reminding us that peacefulness can be a powerful agent for change and renewal.

Focus: Peaceful transformation and renewal.

SACRED WISDOM – NATIVE AMERICAN MEDITATIONS, AFFIRMATIONS, AND REFLECTIONS

April 29

Meditation: Picture the coexistence of various creatures around a tranquil pond, each playing a role in maintaining the balance of the ecosystem. Reflect on the importance of every role in the harmony of life.

Affirmation: I acknowledge and value every role, including my own, understanding that each contributes to the balance and harmony of my community, like the ecosystem of a tranquil pond.

Thought: The pond ecosystem, with its interdependent life forms, teaches us the value of each role in maintaining the balance and health of the whole.

Focus: Valuing roles and community balance.

April 30

Meditation: Envision the resilience of a cactus in the desert, thriving in arid conditions by adapting uniquely to its environment. Let this resilience inspire your own ability to thrive under any circumstances.

Affirmation: I adapt and thrive in all conditions, drawing strength and resilience from within, like a cactus in the desert.

Thought: The cactus, flourishing in the harshest environments, teaches us that with the right adaptations, we too can thrive regardless of challenges.

Focus: Thriving through adaptation and resilience.

May 1

Meditation: Imagine the expanse of a clear night sky filled with stars, each one contributing to the vast tapestry overhead. Let the sense of infinity expand your perspective.

Affirmation: I am part of a vast, interconnected universe, and each connection expands my understanding and sense of belonging, like the stars in the night sky.

Thought: The starry sky, with its infinite expanse, reminds us of our small place within a larger universe, urging us to see beyond our immediate surroundings.

Focus: Expanding perspectives and interconnectedness.

SACRED WISDOM – NATIVE ANERICAN MEDITATIONS, AFFIRMATIONS, AND REFLECTIONS

May 2

Meditation: Reflect on the steady growth of a tree, from a tender sapling to a sturdy oak, each stage crucial and meaningful. Embrace the gradual, steady progress in your own life.

Affirmation: I grow steadily and purposefully, valuing each stage of my development, from sapling to sturdy oak.

Thought: The tree's lifecycle, marked by slow but steady growth, teaches us patience and the importance of each phase in our personal growth.

Focus: Valuing steady growth and patience.

May 3

Meditation: Contemplate the calming motion of clouds drifting across the sky, their shapes ever-changing and adapting. Let this calm adaptability inspire your day.

Affirmation: I embrace adaptability with calmness, allowing my life to shape and reshape like clouds in the sky, smoothly transitioning through changes.

Thought: Clouds, serene and ever-adapting, teach us the beauty of transformation and the peace that can be found in letting go and flowing with change.

Focus: Calm adaptability and transformation.

May 4

Meditation: Picture the dynamic energy of a rushing river, its water clear and powerful. Let the river's unbridled force energize your spirit and guide your actions.

Affirmation: I channel the energy and clarity of a rushing river, moving with purpose and power through life's challenges.

Thought: The rushing river, with its clear and powerful flow, inspires us to move forward with force and clarity, overcoming obstacles with natural momentum.

Focus: Energizing clarity and purposeful action.

SACRED WISDOM – NATIVE AMERICAN MEDITATIONS, AFFIRMATIONS, AND REFLECTIONS

May 5

Meditation: Feel the warmth and brightness of a sunny day, its light invigorating and life-giving. Let this natural brightness uplift your mood and energize your endeavors.

Affirmation: I absorb the sun's energy, allowing its warmth and light to uplift and energize every aspect of my life.

Thought: The sun, a source of light and life, reminds us of the nourishing and uplifting power of positivity and warmth in our lives.

Focus: Upliftment and energy from natural light.

May 6

Meditation: Reflect on the serene beauty of a butterfly garden, where each butterfly flutters independently yet contributes to the garden's harmony. Embrace the beauty of individuality and community.

Affirmation: I celebrate my individuality and contribute to my community, understanding that like butterflies in a garden, we each add unique beauty to the collective.

Thought: The butterfly garden, with its diverse and harmonious inhabitants, teaches us the value of celebrating individuality while contributing to community harmony.

Focus: Individuality within community harmony.

May 7

Meditation: Imagine the soothing sound of rain falling on a forest canopy, each drop nurturing the earth below. Let the rhythmic patter bring a sense of renewal and calm to your spirit.

Affirmation: I welcome renewal and calm with each raindrop, allowing the natural rhythms of life to refresh and restore my spirit.

Thought: The rain's gentle fall on the forest teaches us the beauty of nourishment and renewal, offering peace and new growth to the world.

Focus: Renewal and the calming rhythms of nature.

SACRED WISDOM – NATIVE AMERICAN MEDITATIONS, AFFIRMATIONS, AND REFLECTIONS

May 8

Meditation: Contemplate the vastness of the prairie, its open skies and windswept grasses a testament to freedom and space. Let this expansive view inspire openness and freedom in your thoughts.

Affirmation: I embrace the freedom and openness of the vast prairie, allowing wide-open spaces to expand my thoughts and possibilities.

Thought: The open prairie, with its limitless horizons, teaches us about the freedom that comes with space and the inspiration it offers to our minds.

Focus: Openness and freedom of thought.

May 9

Meditation: Picture the first light of dawn creeping over a mountain peak, slowly illuminating the hidden valleys below. Let this awakening light inspire clarity and enlightenment in your life.

Affirmation: I embrace the clarity and enlightenment of dawn's first light, allowing it to illuminate my path and deepen my understanding of the world around me.

Thought: The dawn light over mountains shows us that enlightenment often comes gradually, revealing the world's beauty and complexity layer by layer.

Focus: Clarity and enlightenment.

May 10

Meditation: Feel the energy of a vibrant city street, where every individual contributes to the dynamic tapestry of urban life. Let this collective energy inspire connectivity and activity in your own life.

Affirmation: I draw energy from the vibrant life around me, engaging actively with my community and contributing to its dynamic flow.

Thought: The energy of a bustling city teaches us about the power of community and the invigorating force of collective human activity.

Focus: Engaging with community and dynamic living.

SACRED WISDOM – NATIVE ANERICAN MEDITATIONS, AFFIRMATIONS, AND REFLECTIONS

May 11

Meditation: Imagine the delicate balance of a spider's web, each thread contributing to a masterpiece of natural engineering. Let this intricate balance inspire meticulous care and precision in your endeavors.

Affirmation: I value precision and care in my actions, weaving my tasks with the meticulousness of a spider's web, each part crucial to the whole.

Thought: The spider's web, with its delicate yet strong structure, teaches us the importance of precision and the strength that comes from careful planning.

Focus: Precision and meticulousness in actions.

May 12

Meditation: Consider the quiet power of the moon influencing the tides from afar, a subtle yet undeniable force. Let this remind you of the strength of quiet influence in your own life.

Affirmation: I wield quiet influence with confidence, understanding the power of subtle forces in shaping the environment and relationships around me.

Thought: The moon's control over the tides, though quiet, is immensely powerful, showing us that influence does not need to be loud to be effective.

Focus: The power of quiet influence.

May 13

Meditation: Reflect on the enduring warmth of an evening campfire, its flames flickering with stories and memories. Let the warmth and light inspire shared moments and connections.

Affirmation: I cherish and cultivate warm connections, sharing stories and experiences around the communal fires of friendship and family.

Thought: The campfire, a gathering place for sharing and warmth, teaches us the value of coming together to share our stories and warmth in community.

Focus: Cultivating connections and shared experiences.

SACRED WISDOM – NATIVE ANERICAN MEDITATIONS, AFFIRMATIONS, AND REFLECTIONS

May 14

Meditation: Visualize a calm sea at twilight, the water reflecting the fading light, offering a mirror to the sky. Let this peaceful reflection inspire inner tranquility and self-reflection.

Affirmation: I reflect on my inner self with tranquility, embracing the calm and clarity that come from introspection, like the sea mirrors the twilight sky.

Thought: The serene sea at twilight teaches us the power of reflection, both in the world and within ourselves, highlighting the importance of calm introspection.

Focus: Inner tranquility and self-reflection.

May 15

Meditation: Consider the gentle unfolding of a fern, each frond slowly revealing its intricate design. Let this natural unveiling inspire patience and appreciation for life's gradual revelations.

Affirmation: I embrace patience and find beauty in gradual revelations, learning from the natural unfolding of life, just as a fern reveals its fronds slowly.

Thought: The fern's growth, gradually unveiling its beauty, teaches us the virtues of patience and the rewards of waiting for natural processes to unfold.

Focus: Patience and appreciation for gradual growth.

May 16

Meditation: Picture the early morning fog enveloping a landscape, softening edges and obscuring the usual views. Let this softened perspective remind you of the benefits of seeing things anew, with less rigidity.

Affirmation: I embrace a softened perspective, allowing myself to see familiar situations with new eyes and less rigidity, as fog alters a landscape.

Thought: Morning fog, with its ability to transform the familiar into something mysterious and new, teaches us the value of flexible perspectives.

Focus: Flexibility and new perspectives.

SACRED WISDOM – NATIVE AMERICAN MEDITATIONS, AFFIRMATIONS, AND REFLECTIONS

May 17

Meditation: Reflect on the rhythm of a heartbeat, steady and reassuring. Let the constancy of your own heart inspire a sense of reliability and steadfastness in your life.

Affirmation: I am steady and reliable, like the rhythm of my heartbeat, providing a constant, reassuring presence in my own life and for those around me.

Thought: The heartbeat, a constant and often unnoticed rhythm, reminds us of the underlying steadiness that guides and supports our entire being.

Focus: Reliability and steadfastness.

May 18

Meditation: Imagine the expansive view from atop a high cliff, overlooking a vast landscape below. Let this broad perspective encourage a bigger picture view of your own life's challenges and opportunities.

Affirmation: I adopt a broad perspective, viewing life's challenges and opportunities from a higher vantage point, gaining wisdom and insight from the expansive view.

Thought: The view from a cliff, with its expansive reach, teaches us to look beyond immediate concerns, considering broader possibilities and contexts.

Focus: Broadening perspectives and insight.

May 19

Meditation: Envision the protective layers of a pine cone, each scale a shield for the seeds within. Let this natural protection inspire you to safeguard your own growth and potential carefully.

Affirmation: I protect and nurture my potential, carefully shielding my growth and aspirations like the scales of a pine cone protect its seeds.

Thought: The pine cone, with its protective scales, teaches us the importance of safeguarding our potential and nurturing our growth until we are ready to flourish.

Focus: Protecting and nurturing personal growth.

SACRED WISDOM – NATIVE ANERICAN MEDITATIONS, AFFIRMATIONS, AND REFLECTIONS

May 20

Meditation: Feel the warmth of the earth after a sunny day, the ground radiating heat back into the evening air. Let this stored warmth remind you of the importance of absorbing and sharing positive energies.

Affirmation: I absorb positivity and warmth throughout my day, radiating it back to others and the world around me, like the earth radiates warmth after the sun sets.

Thought: The warmth of the earth after a day in the sun teaches us about the power of absorbing positive energies and the importance of radiating this warmth outward.

Focus: Absorbing and radiating positivity.

May 21

Meditation: Picture the gentle ascent of morning mist from a river, rising to greet the dawn. Let this graceful rise inspire a sense of calm ascension in your own life.

Affirmation: I rise calmly and gracefully to meet each new day, drawing inspiration from the morning mist's gentle ascent.

Thought: The rising mist teaches us about the quiet, steady lift that comes with new beginnings, urging us to greet each day with grace and tranquility.

Focus: Calm and graceful beginnings.

May 22

Meditation: Reflect on the silent watchfulness of an owl perched high in the night. Embrace the wisdom of observation and the power of silence.

Affirmation: I harness the wisdom found in silence and observation, approaching life's situations with the calm discernment of an owl at night.

Thought: The owl's silent vigilance reminds us of the strength in stillness and the profound insights gained through quiet observation.

Focus: Wisdom in silence and observation.

SACRED WISDOM – NATIVE ANERICAN MEDITATIONS, AFFIRMATIONS, AND REFLECTIONS

May 23

Meditation: Consider the enduring flow of a glacier, slowly shaping the landscape with its immense, quiet power. Let this slow transformation inspire perseverance and impactful change in your life.

Affirmation: I am a force of quiet and persistent change, shaping my world and myself with steady, impactful movements, like a glacier carves the land.

Thought: Glaciers, with their slow yet powerful movement, teach us the potency of perseverance and the significant impact of gradual change.

Focus: Perseverance and gradual impact.

May 24

Meditation: Imagine the vibrant life force of a blooming meadow, buzzing with activity and bursting with color. Let this burst of life invigorate your spirit.

Affirmation: I draw energy from the vitality around me, letting the vibrancy of life invigorate and inspire my daily actions, like a meadow in full bloom.

Thought: The blooming meadow, alive and vibrant, teaches us to embrace the fullness of life, finding energy and inspiration in nature's exuberance.

Focus: Drawing energy from life's vibrancy.

May 25

Meditation: Feel the grounding presence of ancient mountains, their peaks touching the skies. Let their enduring nature inspire stability and a long-term perspective in your life.

Affirmation: I stand firm and grounded, like an ancient mountain, with a perspective that transcends the fleeting troubles of the present.

Thought: Mountains, with their ancient and enduring presence, remind us of the importance of a long-term perspective and the stability it brings.

Focus: Stability and long-term perspective.

SACRED WISDOM – NATIVE ANERICAN MEDITATIONS, AFFIRMATIONS, AND REFLECTIONS

May 26

Meditation: Picture the intricate dance of light and shadow in a forest during sunset, each beam playing through the leaves. Let this interplay inspire a balance of light and dark in your own experiences.

Affirmation: I find balance in the interplay of light and shadow in my life, recognizing that each aspect contributes to a fuller understanding and appreciation of the whole.

Thought: The dance of light and shadow in a forest teaches us that both elements are essential for depth and beauty, urging us to embrace the contrasts in our lives.

Focus: Embracing life's contrasts.

May 27

Meditation: Consider the resilience of a river stone, shaped by the relentless flow of water yet smooth and strong. Let this resilience and adaptation to forces inspire your path.

Affirmation: I am resilient and adaptable, shaped by life's challenges into a smooth, strong presence, like a river stone polished by currents.

Thought: The river stone, with its smoothness earned through enduring resilience, teaches us the beauty and strength that come from facing life's persistent flows.

Focus: Resilience and adaptation.

May 28

Meditation: Visualize the expansive, star-filled night sky stretching endlessly above. Let the vastness of the universe inspire a sense of wonder and possibility in your life.

Affirmation: I embrace the vast possibilities of my life, inspired by the endless expanse of the night sky, feeling connected to the universe's infinite wonder.

Thought: The vastness of the night sky reminds us of the limitless possibilities within and around us, urging us to explore beyond our perceived limits.

Focus: Wonder and exploration of possibilities.

SACRED WISDOM – NATIVE ANERICAN MEDITATIONS, AFFIRMATIONS, AND REFLECTIONS

May 29

Meditation: Reflect on the calmness of a deep ocean, its surface a mirror to the sky yet hiding depths untold. Let the ocean's depth inspire introspection and the exploration of your inner world.

Affirmation: I delve into the depths of my inner self with calm introspection, like the ocean's deep waters, discovering hidden strengths and treasures within.

Thought: The deep ocean, serene yet profound, teaches us the value of looking beneath the surface, exploring our inner depths for greater self-understanding.

Focus: Introspection and self-discovery.

May 30

Meditation: Imagine the gentle touch of a breeze on a warm day, its subtle movement cooling and refreshing. Let this gentle change inspire subtle transformations in your own life.

Affirmation: I welcome gentle changes, allowing the soft breezes of transformation to refresh and renew my spirit, bringing subtle yet impactful shifts.

Thought: The soft touch of a breeze teaches us that not all changes need to be forceful; subtle shifts can also bring significant refreshment and renewal.

Focus: Embracing gentle change.

May 31

Meditation: Consider the steadfastness of a lighthouse, standing firm against the storm, guiding safely in darkness. Let this symbol of guidance and protection inspire you to be a beacon in your own and others' lives.

Affirmation: I stand as a beacon of guidance and protection, steadfast and sure, offering light in the darkness for myself and those around me.

Thought: The lighthouse, enduring and reliable, reminds us of the importance of being a steadfast source of guidance and safety for others.

Focus: Being a guiding light.

SACRED WISDOM – NATIVE ANERICAN MEDITATIONS, AFFIRMATIONS, AND REFLECTIONS

June 1

Meditation: Picture the early morning dew glistening on a spider's web, each droplet reflecting the light. Let this natural artistry inspire appreciation for life's delicate balances and intricate designs.

Affirmation: I appreciate and seek the delicate balances and intricate designs in life, recognizing the beauty and complexity in nature's artistry.

Thought: The dew-covered spider's web, intricate and delicate, teaches us to notice and cherish the fine and complex balances that make up our world.

Focus: Appreciation for complexity and balance.

June 2

Meditation: Reflect on the journey of a river from mountain to ocean, its course natural and determined. Let this journey inspire perseverance and purpose in your path through life.

Affirmation: I navigate my life with the purpose and perseverance of a river, flowing naturally yet resolutely toward my goals, adapting and overcoming obstacles along the way.

Thought: The river's journey, adapting yet persistent, teaches us the power of moving towards our goals with inherent purpose and adaptability.

Focus: Purpose and perseverance in life's journey.

June 3

Meditation: Envision the growth of a seed into a towering tree, each stage critical to its development. Let this natural progression inspire growth and development in your own life.

Affirmation: I embrace each stage of my growth, recognizing that like a tree, every phase builds upon the last, contributing to my strength and stature.

Thought: The growth of a tree, from seed to towering presence, reminds us of the continual, layered development necessary to achieve mature strength and beauty.

Focus: Embracing and nurturing personal growth.

SACRED WISDOM – NATIVE AMERICAN MEDITATIONS, AFFIRMATIONS, AND REFLECTIONS

June 4

Meditation: Imagine the warmth of the sun at noon, its rays directly illuminating and energizing the earth. Let this direct and powerful energy inspire a focused and vibrant approach in your life.

Affirmation: I harness the sun's powerful energy, focusing it to illuminate and energize my endeavors, driving me forward with clarity and purpose.

Thought: The sun at its zenith provides not just light but powerful energy, reminding us of the potential within us to focus our efforts and achieve great things.

Focus: Energizing focus and clarity.

June 5

Meditation: Reflect on the lifecycle of a butterfly, from caterpillar to cocoon to beautiful winged creature. Let this transformation inspire your personal evolution and the embracing of change.

Affirmation: I embrace transformation with grace, allowing each stage of my life to evolve naturally and beautifully, like the metamorphosis of a butterfly.

Thought: The butterfly's journey is a powerful symbol of transformation, teaching us that significant changes involve growth and renewal at every stage.

Focus: Embracing transformation and renewal.

June 6

Meditation: Picture the rhythmic pattern of waves crashing and retreating on the shore. Let the constant rhythm of these natural cycles remind you of the ebb and flow in your own life.

Affirmation: I am at peace with the ebb and flow of my life, understanding that like the waves, each cycle has its purpose and brings balance.

Thought: Waves, with their ceaseless rhythms of advance and retreat, teach us about the natural cycles of coming and going, each contributing to life's balance.

Focus: Accepting life's natural rhythms.

SACRED WISDOM – NATIVE ANERICAN MEDITATIONS, AFFIRMATIONS, AND REFLECTIONS

June 7

Meditation: Consider the solitude of a mountain peak, standing above the world in quiet majesty. Let this solitude inspire a sense of inner peace and self-reliance.

Affirmation: I find strength in solitude, standing firm and tranquil like a mountain peak, drawing peace from my inner self.

Thought: The solitude of a mountain peak, removed from the noise below, teaches us the value of finding peace and strength within ourselves.

Focus: Inner peace and strength in solitude.

June 8

Meditation: Imagine the crackle of a campfire, the flames flickering with life and warmth. Let this comforting presence inspire warmth and light in your interactions with others.

Affirmation: I bring warmth and light to my interactions, like a campfire in the night, providing comfort and connection to those around me.

Thought: The campfire, a gathering place of warmth and light, reminds us of the importance of being a source of comfort and brightness in others' lives.

Focus: Providing warmth and light in relationships.

June 9

Meditation: Picture the early morning fog clearing as the sun rises, revealing the landscape's details. Let this gradual clearing inspire clarity and revelation in your own understanding.

Affirmation: I welcome clarity as I navigate my day, allowing the sun's rising light to clear the fog over my thoughts, revealing a sharp and bright understanding.

Thought: The dispersing fog at sunrise teaches us about the arrival of clarity and the revealing power of light, urging us to seek understanding as the day unfolds.

Focus: Clarity and understanding.

SACRED WISDOM – NATIVE ANERICAN MEDITATIONS, AFFIRMATIONS, AND REFLECTIONS

June 10

Meditation: Reflect on the silent growth of a night-blooming flower, its petals unfolding under the moonlight. Let this quiet, unnoticed growth inspire acknowledgment of your unseen efforts.

Affirmation: I recognize and value the silent, unseen efforts in my growth, understanding that like the night-blooming flower, much happens beneath the surface.

Thought: The night-blooming flower, unfolding quietly and unseen, teaches us that significant growth often occurs out of sight, deserving recognition and appreciation.

Focus: Valuing unseen growth and efforts.

June 11

Meditation: Visualize the peaceful expanse of a still lake at dawn, its surface a perfect mirror reflecting the sky. Let this tranquil scene inspire a sense of peace and reflection in your life.

Affirmation: I embrace the stillness within me, reflecting peace and tranquility in my thoughts and actions, just as the lake reflects the sky at dawn.

Thought: The still lake at dawn, with its serene reflections, teaches us the value of calmness and the clarity that comes from peaceful introspection.

Focus: Inner peace and reflective calm.

June 12

Meditation: Consider the enduring presence of an old tree, its roots deep and branches high. Let this symbol of strength and resilience inspire steadiness and growth in your life.

Affirmation: I am rooted in strength and resilience, growing steadily towards my goals, supported by a foundation as strong as an ancient tree.

Thought: The old tree, enduring through seasons and storms, teaches us the importance of deep roots and the steady growth they enable.

Focus: Strength, resilience, and steady growth.

SACRED WISDOM – NATIVE AMERICAN MEDITATIONS, AFFIRMATIONS, AND REFLECTIONS

June 13

Meditation: Picture the gentle unfolding of a rose, each petal opening at its own pace. Let this natural timing inspire patience and trust in your own processes of development.

Affirmation: I trust in the timing of my own growth, patiently unfolding like a rose, each phase revealing its own beauty and purpose.

Thought: The rose's unfolding teaches us that growth is a gradual process, each stage essential and not to be rushed, reflecting the beauty of natural development.

Focus: Patience and trusting natural timing.

June 14

Meditation: Imagine the rhythmic pounding of rain on the earth during a thunderstorm, each drop revitalizing the soil. Let this invigorating force inspire renewal and vigor in your life.

Affirmation: I welcome renewal with each challenge I face, allowing life's storms to revitalize and strengthen me, just as rain nourishes the earth.

Thought: The thunderstorm, with its powerful rain, reminds us that intense experiences can bring renewal and growth, nourishing our spirits like rain does the earth.

Focus: Renewal through challenges.

June 15

Meditation: Reflect on the intricate web of an ecosystem, each component interdependent and crucial. Let this complexity inspire awareness of your own connections and impacts within your community.

Affirmation: I acknowledge and value my role within the larger community, understanding my interdependence and the impact of my actions, like each element in an ecosystem.

Thought: The ecosystem, with its delicate balances and interdependencies, teaches us the importance of each individual's role in maintaining the health of the whole.

Focus: Awareness of interdependence and community impact.

SACRED WISDOM – NATIVE AMERICAN MEDITATIONS, AFFIRMATIONS, AND REFLECTIONS

June 16

Meditation: Picture the quiet majesty of a snowy landscape under the moonlight, its silence profound and enveloping. Let this peaceful stillness inspire a sense of clarity and calm in your endeavors.

Affirmation: I find clarity and peace in the stillness of my mind, embracing the quiet majesty of a clear, moonlit night to guide my thoughts and actions.

Thought: The snowy landscape at night, peaceful and undisturbed, teaches us the power of stillness in bringing clarity and serenity to our minds.

Focus: Clarity and peace through stillness.

June 17

Meditation: Consider the burst of life in a meadow at sunrise, each creature and plant awakening with the light. Let this daily renewal inspire a fresh start and positive outlook each morning.

Affirmation: I embrace each day with a fresh start, inspired by the daily renewal of a meadow at sunrise, welcoming opportunities and positivity with each new light.

Thought: The meadow at sunrise, alive with activity and renewal, reminds us of the endless possibilities each new day holds, inspiring us to greet each morning with optimism.

Focus: Fresh starts and daily renewal.

June 18

Meditation: Imagine the harmonious song of a forest, each creature contributing its voice to the symphony of life. Let this unity inspire cooperation and harmony in your own interactions.

Affirmation: I contribute to the harmony of my surroundings, adding my voice to the collective melody, creating beautiful symphonies in collaboration with others.

Thought: The forest symphony, with its diverse contributions, teaches us the beauty of unity in diversity and the strength of cooperative endeavors.

Focus: Harmony and cooperation in diversity.

SACRED WISDOM – NATIVE ANERICAN MEDITATIONS, AFFIRMATIONS, AND REFLECTIONS

June 19

Meditation: Visualize the enduring rhythm of the waves crashing against the shore, each one unique yet part of a continuous pattern. Let this remind you of the importance of consistency and persistence in your pursuits.

Affirmation: I embrace persistence and consistency in my actions, like the rhythmic waves that shape the shore, knowing that steady efforts yield significant results.

Thought: The ceaseless waves, shaping coasts and cliffs, exemplify the transformative power of persistence and the importance of steady, consistent efforts.

Focus: Persistence and consistency in action.

June 20

Meditation: Reflect on the warmth of a summer solstice, the sun reaching its highest point, bathing the earth in light and energy. Let this peak of sunlight invigorate your spirit and ambitions.

Affirmation: I am energized and uplifted by the peak sunlight of the summer solstice, using this high point to fuel my ambitions and brighten my outlook.

Thought: The summer solstice, a time of maximum light and energy, encourages us to harness this peak moment to energize our lives and ambitions.

Focus: Harnessing energy for personal growth.

June 21

Meditation: Picture the intricate patterns formed by frost on a window, each a unique masterpiece of natural art. Let the beauty of these transient patterns inspire an appreciation for fleeting moments.

Affirmation: I appreciate the beauty in fleeting moments, understanding that like frost patterns, they are precious and unique, to be cherished while they last.

Thought: Frost patterns, beautiful yet temporary, teach us to value the impermanence of moments and find beauty in transience.

Focus: Appreciation of fleeting beauty.

June 22

Meditation: Imagine the strength and stability of a stone arch, naturally formed over millennia. Let this structure inspire resilience and the understanding that time and persistence can create enduring beauty and strength.

Affirmation: I build resilience and stability in my life, knowing that over time, my persistent efforts will form a strong, beautiful foundation, like a stone arch.

Thought: The stone arch, crafted by nature's patient artistry, reminds us of the strength and beauty that result from resilience and the passage of time.

Focus: Building resilience and enduring beauty.

June 23

Meditation: Consider the coolness of a deep forest shade on a hot day, providing relief and a respite from the sun's intensity. Let this natural shelter inspire you to find and provide relief in challenging times.

Affirmation: I seek and provide shelter in life's challenges, offering relief and comfort, just as the forest shade offers a cool respite from the heat.

Thought: The cooling shade of a forest not only provides relief but also represents the sanctuary that can be found and shared during life's more intense periods.

Focus: Providing and finding relief.

June 24

Meditation: Reflect on the silent flight of an owl at night, moving effortlessly through the dark, guided by keen senses. Let this effective navigation inspire confidence and trust in your abilities to maneuver through challenges.

Affirmation: I navigate challenges with the silent confidence of an owl in flight, trusting my instincts and abilities to guide me smoothly through the dark.

Thought: The owl's silent, effective flight through the night teaches us about the power of quiet confidence and the importance of trusting our inner senses when facing challenges.

Focus: Confidence and trust in abilities.

SACRED WISDOM – NATIVE ANERICAN MEDITATIONS, AFFIRMATIONS, AND REFLECTIONS

June 25

Meditation: Visualize the first light of dawn spreading across a tranquil sea, the gentle hues of morning painting the sky and water. Let the calm and beauty of this scene inspire serenity and a fresh perspective for the day.

Affirmation: I welcome each day with the serenity of dawn, allowing the fresh start to paint my thoughts with peaceful colors and clarity.

Thought: The tranquil dawn over the sea reminds us of the peace and beauty that can begin each day, urging us to adopt a serene and clear perspective.

Focus: Serenity and fresh perspectives.

June 26

Meditation: Reflect on the way a river carves its path through the landscape, persistently and sometimes imperceptibly shaping the earth. Let this natural persistence inspire determination and subtle influence in your own life.

Affirmation: I shape my world with steady determination, like the river shapes its course, understanding the power of persistent, gentle influence.

Thought: The river, with its quiet yet powerful reshaping of the landscape, teaches us the effectiveness of patience and persistence in achieving long-term goals.

Focus: Persistence and subtle influence.

June 27

Meditation: Imagine the soft rustle of leaves in a gentle breeze, each movement contributing to a soothing symphony. Let this harmonious sound encourage peace and harmony in your interactions.

Affirmation: I engage with the world in harmony, like leaves rustling peacefully in the breeze, contributing to life's gentle symphony with my actions.

Thought: The rustling leaves, a simple yet profound sound, remind us of the beauty of peaceful coexistence and the symphony we create together.

Focus: Harmony and peaceful interactions.

SACRED WISDOM – NATIVE AMERICAN MEDITATIONS, AFFIRMATIONS, AND REFLECTIONS

June 28

Meditation: Picture the robust growth of a summer garden, bursting with life and color. Let the vibrancy and diversity of the garden inspire a rich and flourishing life.

Affirmation: I cultivate a life as vibrant and diverse as a summer garden, nurturing growth and celebrating the abundance around me.

Thought: A summer garden, with its riot of colors and life, teaches us to nurture our own lives with care and to celebrate the abundance that diversity brings.

Focus: Vibrancy and nurturing growth.

June 29

Meditation: Consider the quiet majesty of a full moon illuminating the night sky, its light casting serene shadows and turning the familiar into the magical. Let this transformation inspire a sense of wonder and a new vision in your life.

Affirmation: I embrace the transformative light of understanding, letting it reveal the wonder in the ordinary and guide my vision to see the magical in the everyday.

Thought: The full moon's light, transforming night landscapes into scenes of serene beauty, reminds us of the power of perspective and the wonder that comes with seeing things anew.

Focus: Transformation and renewed vision.

June 30

Meditation: Visualize the energetic leap of a salmon upstream, its body surging against the current in a display of strength and determination. Let this powerful struggle inspire resilience and courage in your own challenges.

Affirmation: I meet my challenges with the resilience and determination of a salmon swimming upstream, using my strength to overcome obstacles and reach my goals.

Thought: The salmon's upstream journey is a testament to natural resilience and determination, encouraging us to face our own challenges with similar vigor.

Focus: Resilience and overcoming obstacles.

SACRED WISDOM – NATIVE ANERICAN MEDITATIONS, AFFIRMATIONS, AND REFLECTIONS

July 1

Meditation: Imagine the refreshing coolness of a mountain stream on a hot day, its clear waters soothing and revitalizing. Let this natural refreshment inspire renewal and a cooling of passions or stress in your life.

Affirmation: I seek and embrace moments of refreshment and renewal, like the cool waters of a mountain stream, soothing my spirit and calming my stress.

Thought: The mountain stream, with its refreshing coolness, teaches us the value of natural pauses for renewal, reminding us to periodically refresh our spirits.

Focus: Refreshment and calming renewal.

July 2

Meditation: Picture the endless expanse of a desert under the blazing sun, its vastness both daunting and inspiring. Let the resilience of life that thrives there inspire your own perseverance and adaptability.

Affirmation: I embody the resilience and adaptability of life in the desert, thriving in all conditions with strength and perseverance.

Thought: The desert, with its harsh conditions yet thriving life, teaches us the power of adaptation and the strength found in resilience against adversity.

Focus: Resilience and adaptability.

July 3

Meditation: Visualize the peacefulness of twilight as day slowly transitions to night, the sky painted with hues of pink and purple. Let this peaceful change inspire tranquility and a smooth transition in your own life changes.

Affirmation: I embrace life's transitions with the tranquility of twilight, calmly and beautifully shifting from one phase to the next.

Thought: Twilight, with its serene and beautiful transition, reminds us that change can be peaceful and stunning, encouraging us to approach transitions with a calm heart.

Focus: Tranquil transitions and serenity.

SACRED WISDOM – NATIVE ANERICAN MEDITATIONS, AFFIRMATIONS, AND REFLECTIONS

July 4

Meditation: Imagine the explosive joy of fireworks lighting up the night sky, each burst a celebration of light and color. Let this vibrant display inspire joy and a celebratory spirit in your life.

Affirmation: I celebrate each moment with joy and vibrancy, like fireworks in the night sky, lighting up my life with spectacular moments of happiness.

Thought: Fireworks, a symbol of celebration and joy, remind us to embrace the spectacular and joyful moments in life, celebrating them with exuberance.

Focus: Celebrating joy and life's highlights.

July 5

Meditation: Consider the steadfast growth of ivy up a wall, steadily climbing and expanding its reach. Let this persistent growth inspire steady progress and expansion in your personal or professional goals.

Affirmation: I grow and expand steadily, like ivy climbing a wall, persistently moving towards my goals with determination and resilience.

Thought: Ivy, with its relentless growth and ability to overcome obstacles, teaches us the virtues of persistence and the steady progress towards achieving our ambitions.

Focus: Persistent growth and goal achievement.

July 6

Meditation: Reflect on the calm that descends with a gentle snowfall, each flake silently adding to a blanket of tranquility. Let this quiet accumulation inspire peace and a methodical approach in your endeavors.

Affirmation: I approach my endeavors with the calm and methodical nature of falling snow, accumulating success quietly but surely.

Thought: The gentle snowfall, with its quiet and steady accumulation, teaches us that silent and consistent efforts can lead to significant impacts over time.

Focus: Peaceful persistence and impact.

SACRED WISDOM – NATIVE ANERICAN MEDITATIONS, AFFIRMATIONS, AND REFLECTIONS

July 7

Meditation: Visualize the early morning fog lifting over a lake, slowly revealing the clear waters beneath. Let this gradual unveiling inspire clarity and new understanding in your thoughts and perceptions.

Affirmation: I welcome clarity and understanding, as gradual and refreshing as the lifting fog over a lake, revealing insights and truths beneath.

Thought: The lifting fog, revealing the landscape bit by bit, reminds us that clarity often comes gradually, providing fresh insights as it clears.

Focus: Gaining clarity and understanding.

July 8

Meditation: Picture the intricate dance of a campfire's flames, flickering and weaving unpredictably. Let the fire's lively and spontaneous movement inspire flexibility and spontaneity in your life.

Affirmation: I embrace flexibility and spontaneity, inspired by the lively dance of campfire flames, adapting and thriving in the unpredictable flows of life.

Thought: The campfire, with its spontaneous and vibrant flames, teaches us to appreciate and adapt to the unpredictability of life, finding joy in spontaneity.

Focus: Embracing flexibility and spontaneity.

July 9

Meditation: Imagine the stillness of an early morning forest, the silence broken only by the soft calls of birds. Let the quietude and awakening nature inspire a peaceful start to your day.

Affirmation: I embrace the peace of the morning, allowing the quiet awakening of nature to ground and center my thoughts as I start my day.

Thought: The tranquil forest at dawn, with its gentle stirrings of life, teaches us the beauty of starting the day in peace, setting a calm tone for all that follows.

Focus: Peaceful beginnings and morning tranquility.

SACRED WISDOM – NATIVE ANERICAN MEDITATIONS, AFFIRMATIONS, AND REFLECTIONS

July 10

Meditation: Reflect on the steady erosion of a mountain by wind and water over centuries. Let this natural, gradual transformation inspire patience and understanding of the slow but inevitable changes in life.

Affirmation: I accept the slow and steady changes in my life with patience, understanding that, like a mountain shaped by elements, time brings transformation.

Thought: The erosion of a mountain, though slow, results in dramatic landscapes, reminding us that patience can lead to significant and beautiful changes over time.

Focus: Patience and gradual transformation.

July 11

Meditation: Picture the joyful flight of a flock of birds, each moving in harmony with the others. Let this collective coordination inspire teamwork and unity in your interactions.

Affirmation: I move in harmony with those around me, embracing teamwork and unity, as birds in flight rely on each other to navigate and soar.

Thought: The synchronized flight of birds teaches us the power of teamwork and the beauty of moving in unity, achieving more together than alone.

Focus: Teamwork and harmonious interactions.

July 12

Meditation: Imagine the first crack of lightning in a storm, sudden and powerful. Let this burst of energy inspire decisive action and the power of a clear, impactful decision in your life.

Affirmation: I harness the decisive power of lightning, making clear and impactful decisions that illuminate and transform my path forward.

Thought: Lightning, with its sudden and powerful strike, teaches us about the impact of decisiveness and the clarity that can come from a bold, swift action.

Focus: Decisiveness and impactful actions.

SACRED WISDOM – NATIVE ANERICAN MEDITATIONS, AFFIRMATIONS, AND REFLECTIONS

July 13

Meditation: Consider the slow opening of a lotus flower on the water, each petal unfolding at its own pace. Let this gentle opening inspire a measured and mindful approach to personal growth.

Affirmation: I unfold at my own pace, embracing each stage of my growth with mindfulness and grace, like a lotus flower revealing its beauty slowly.

Thought: The lotus flower, blooming slowly and beautifully, reminds us of the dignity in gradual development and the importance of each growth stage.

Focus: Mindful and gradual personal growth.

July 14

Meditation: Visualize the ebb and flow of the tides, controlled by the moon's pull. Let this natural rhythm remind you of the need to give and take in your life, balancing your efforts with rest.

Affirmation: I balance my efforts with rest, embracing the natural ebb and flow of my energies, like the tides guided by the moon.

Thought: The rhythmic tides, ebbing and flowing under lunar influence, teach us the importance of balance in our exertions and the restorative power of rest.

Focus: Balance of effort and rest.

July 15

Meditation: Reflect on the warmth of a summer's day, its sunlight nurturing the earth. Let this nurturing warmth inspire you to care for and uplift those around you.

Affirmation: I spread warmth and nurturing care, uplifting those around me with kindness and support, just as the sun nurtures life on earth.

Thought: The nurturing warmth of the sun, essential for life, reminds us of the importance of kindness and support in fostering growth and well-being in our communities.

Focus: Nurturing and uplifting others.

SACRED WISDOM – NATIVE ANERICAN MEDITATIONS, AFFIRMATIONS, AND REFLECTIONS

July 16

Meditation: Imagine the slow, graceful drift of clouds across the sky, constantly changing shape and direction. Let this fluid motion inspire adaptability and the acceptance of change in your life.

Affirmation: I embrace change with the grace of drifting clouds, adapting fluidly to life's shifts and embracing new shapes and paths as they come.

Thought: The ever-changing clouds remind us that nothing is static, teaching us to accept and adapt to change with elegance and ease.

Focus: Adaptability and acceptance of change.

July 17

Meditation: Reflect on the enduring presence of rocks along a shoreline, shaped over millennia by the sea. Let their smoothed surfaces inspire resilience and a long-term perspective on challenges and transformations.

Affirmation: I stand resilient like shoreline rocks, letting life's challenges smooth and shape me over time, contributing to my strength and character.

Thought: Shoreline rocks, shaped by the relentless sea, exemplify the beauty of resilience and the transformative power of persistent challenges.

Focus: Resilience and transformation through challenges.

July 18

Meditation: Picture the early dew on grass at sunrise, each droplet catching the light and sparkling. Let this refreshing scene inspire purity and a fresh start in your approach to each day.

Affirmation: I start each day refreshed and pure, like morning dew, embracing new beginnings with clarity and sparkle.

Thought: Morning dew, fresh and sparkling at sunrise, teaches us the value of starting anew each day, with clarity and freshness infusing our actions.

Focus: Fresh starts and daily renewal.

July 19

Meditation: Consider the calm yet powerful flow of a deep river, its currents hidden beneath a tranquil surface. Let this depth and power inspire inner strength and calm assertiveness in your life.

Affirmation: I channel deep inner strength and calm assertiveness, moving through life with the quiet power and depth of a flowing river.

Thought: The deep river, calm on the surface yet powerful beneath, teaches us the strength of subtlety and the impact of understated power.

Focus: Inner strength and calm assertiveness.

July 20

Meditation: Imagine the vast, open plains stretching under a wide sky, offering space and freedom. Let this openness inspire expansiveness in your thinking and possibilities.

Affirmation: I embrace the openness of the plains, allowing my thoughts and possibilities to expand under the wide sky, free from constraints.

Thought: The open plains, boundless and free, remind us of the limitless potential in our lives when we allow our thoughts to roam wide and free.

Focus: Expansiveness in thinking and possibilities.

July 21

Meditation: Visualize a starry night sky, each star a point of light in the vast darkness. Let this cosmic perspective inspire wonder and a sense of connection to something greater than yourself.

Affirmation: I connect with the wonder and vastness of the universe, each star reminding me of my part in a larger cosmic story.

Thought: The starry sky, vast and dotted with countless lights, teaches us about our small yet significant place in the universe, inspiring awe and connectivity.

Focus: Cosmic wonder and connectivity.

SACRED WISDOM – NATIVE AMERICAN MEDITATIONS, AFFIRMATIONS, AND REFLECTIONS

July 22

Meditation: Reflect on the layers of a mountain, each stratum telling a story of eras past. Let these layers inspire a historical perspective on your life, understanding each phase as part of a larger story.

Affirmation: I view my life as layers of a mountain, each phase a rich stratum that adds depth and history, contributing to the whole of my existence.

Thought: The layered mountain, with its historical strata, teaches us to appreciate the depth and history in our lives, each layer adding to our personal narrative.

Focus: Historical perspective and appreciation of life's layers.

July 23

Meditation: Picture the quiet beauty of a forest at night, the moonlight filtering through the trees, casting gentle shadows. Let the stillness and the play of light and dark inspire introspection and peace.

Affirmation: I find peace in stillness, drawing insight from the quiet beauty of the night, as moonlight dances through the forest of my thoughts.

Thought: The serene forest at night, illuminated subtly by moonlight, teaches us the beauty of tranquility and the depth that can be found in stillness.

Focus: Peaceful introspection and the beauty of stillness.

July 24

Meditation: Reflect on the cycle of the seasons, each bringing its own challenges and gifts. Let this natural progression inspire acceptance and appreciation for the varied phases in your life.

Affirmation: I embrace each season of my life, recognizing the unique challenges and gifts each brings, just as nature cycles through its seasons.

Thought: The unending cycle of seasons, each with its own essence, reminds us to accept and find beauty in every phase of our lives, recognizing the importance of change and renewal.

Focus: Acceptance and appreciation of life's seasons.

SACRED WISDOM – NATIVE AMERICAN MEDITATIONS, AFFIRMATIONS, AND REFLECTIONS

July 25

Meditation: Imagine the ripple effect created by a single pebble thrown into a still pond. Let the impact of small actions inspire you to initiate positive change, knowing even small efforts can have far-reaching effects.

Affirmation: I recognize the power of small actions, initiating change with the confidence that even a single ripple can spread widely across the pond of life.

Thought: The ripple effect from a single pebble shows us that small beginnings can lead to significant impacts, encouraging us to never underestimate our actions.

Focus: The power of small actions and positive change.

July 26

Meditation: Visualize the expanse of a clear blue sky, unobstructed and open. Let this boundless view inspire a mindset of unlimited possibilities and freedom from limitations.

Affirmation: I embrace a mindset of boundless possibilities, inspired by the vastness of the clear blue sky, feeling free from limitations and open to opportunities.

Thought: The open sky, vast and limitless, teaches us about the potential that lies in an unbounded perspective, encouraging us to think broadly and without constraint.

Focus: Unlimited possibilities and freedom from limitations.

July 27

Meditation: Picture the steadfast growth of a coral reef, each organism contributing to a larger, vibrant ecosystem. Let this collective thriving inspire community and cooperation in your own circles.

Affirmation: I contribute to and thrive within my community, recognizing that like a coral reef, each of us plays a vital role in creating a vibrant collective ecosystem.

Thought: The coral reef, with its diverse and interdependent organisms, teaches us the strength of community and the beauty of cooperative existence.

Focus: Community cooperation and collective thriving.

SACRED WISDOM – NATIVE AMERICAN MEDITATIONS, AFFIRMATIONS, AND REFLECTIONS

July 28

Meditation: Consider the powerful force of a waterfall, water cascading down with relentless energy and beauty. Let this natural power inspire strength and relentless pursuit of your passions.

Affirmation: I harness the strength and beauty of a waterfall, pursuing my goals with relentless energy and a powerful presence.

Thought: The waterfall, with its powerful and ceaseless flow, serves as a reminder of the strength in persistence and the beauty in pursuing our passions with vigor.

Focus: Strength and relentless pursuit of passions.

July 29

Meditation: Reflect on the warmth of a summer evening, the air soft and the world quieting down. Let the calmness of summer nights inspire relaxation and a soothing end to your daily endeavors.

Affirmation: I embrace the calmness of summer evenings, allowing the soft end of each day to bring relaxation and peace to my soul.

Thought: Summer evenings, with their gentle warmth and calming atmosphere, teach us the importance of unwinding and relaxing after the day's activities, nurturing our well-being.

Focus: Relaxation and peaceful endings.

July 30

Meditation: Imagine the first light of dawn peeking through a dense forest, the beams of sunlight finding their way through the trees. Let this gentle illumination inspire hope and new beginnings in your life.

Affirmation: I welcome each new day with hope, allowing the first light of dawn to illuminate my path and guide my steps with new possibilities.

Thought: The dawning light through a forest teaches us that no matter how dense the obstacles, the light of new beginnings will always find a way through.

Focus: Hope and new beginnings.

SACRED WISDOM – NATIVE ANERICAN MEDITATIONS, AFFIRMATIONS, AND REFLECTIONS

July 31

Meditation: Reflect on the peaceful motion of clouds drifting across a summer sky, their shapes and speeds ever-changing. Let this peaceful and constant change inspire adaptability and calm in your own transformations.

Affirmation: I embrace change with the calmness of drifting clouds, adapting seamlessly to life's shifts and finding beauty in transformation.

Thought: Clouds, ever-changing yet serene, teach us that change can be graceful and peaceful, inspiring us to approach life's transformations with a calm adaptability.

Focus: Adaptability and peace in change.

August 1

Meditation: Picture the robust life of a bustling beehive, each bee contributing to the success of the whole. Let this example of teamwork and diligence inspire your own efforts and collaborations.

Affirmation: I value and contribute to teamwork with the diligence of a bee, understanding that every effort supports the greater good of the community.

Thought: The beehive, a model of efficiency and cooperation, reminds us of the power of collective effort and the importance of each individual's contributions.

Focus: Teamwork and collective diligence.

August 2

Meditation: Visualize a mountain stream cascading over rocks, its water clear and pure. Let the clarity and purity of this stream inspire transparency and honesty in your interactions.

Affirmation: I strive for clarity and honesty in all my interactions, inspired by the pure and transparent flow of a mountain stream.

Thought: The mountain stream, with its clear and straightforward course, teaches us the value of being clear and pure in our intentions and interactions.

SACRED WISDOM – NATIVE AMERICAN MEDITATIONS, AFFIRMATIONS, AND REFLECTIONS

Focus: Clarity and honesty.

August 3

Meditation: Consider the silent growth of a tree at night, absorbing the cool, moist air. Let this quiet, unseen progress inspire recognition of the subtle yet significant growth in your own life.

Affirmation: I acknowledge and appreciate the subtle growths in my life, understanding that significant changes often happen quietly and incrementally.

Thought: The tree's growth at night, silent and unseen, reminds us that growth is not always loud or visible, often occurring quietly yet profoundly.

Focus: Recognizing subtle growth.

August 4

Meditation: Picture the intricate weaving of a spider's web, each thread essential to the whole. Let this intricate craftsmanship inspire attention to detail and the interconnectedness of your own projects and relationships.

Affirmation: I weave my projects and relationships with care and precision, recognizing that each detail is crucial to the strength and beauty of the whole.

Thought: The spider's web, with its detailed and precise construction, teaches us the importance of attention to detail and how every part contributes to the whole.

Focus: Attention to detail and interconnectedness.

August 5

Meditation: Reflect on the rhythm of waves lapping at the shore under a full moon, their sound steady and soothing. Let this natural rhythm bring a sense of peace and regularity to your life.

Affirmation: I find peace in life's natural rhythms, allowing the steady cadence of waves under the moonlight to soothe and stabilize my spirit.

Thought: The rhythmic waves under the moonlight, constant and soothing, teach us the calming power of nature's rhythms, encouraging us to incorporate this steadiness into our lives.

Focus: Peace and steadiness through natural rhythms.

August 6

Meditation: Imagine the serene beauty of a butterfly garden at sunrise, the light gently waking each creature. Let this peaceful awakening inspire a gentle start to your day, filled with beauty and calm.

Affirmation: I embrace each new morning with the serenity of a sunrise in a butterfly garden, allowing the gentle beginning to fill my day with peace and beauty.

Thought: The quiet of a garden at sunrise, as it awakens to life, teaches us the beauty of starting the day calmly, which can set a peaceful tone for all that follows.

Focus: Gentle beginnings and peaceful starts.

August 7

Meditation: Reflect on the powerful presence of a thunderstorm, its energy undeniable and transformative. Let the strength and renewal brought by the storm inspire resilience and rejuvenation in your life.

Affirmation: I draw strength from life's storms, using their energy for personal renewal and emerging more resilient and revitalized.

Thought: Thunderstorms, while powerful and sometimes daunting, bring essential water and renewal, reminding us that challenges often precede significant growth.

Focus: Resilience and renewal through challenges.

August 8

Meditation: Visualize a clear, starlit night on a quiet beach, the stars' reflections twinkling in the gentle surf. Let the vastness of the night sky over the sea inspire a sense of perspective and infinite possibilities.

Affirmation: I am open to the infinite possibilities that surround me, inspired by the vastness of the starlit sea, and the perspective it provides.

Thought: The expanse of the night sky over the ocean reminds us of the vastness of our own potential and the endless possibilities that life offers.

Focus: Expanding perspectives and embracing possibilities.

August 9

Meditation: Consider the layered petals of a blooming rose, each layer revealing more depth and beauty. Let the complexity and depth of the rose inspire a deeper understanding and appreciation of life's complexities.

Affirmation: I appreciate the depth and complexity in my life, seeing each layer as part of a beautiful whole, much like the petals of a blooming rose.

Thought: The rose, with its intricate layers, teaches us to see the beauty in life's complexities and to appreciate the richness they bring to our experiences.

Focus: Appreciating complexity and depth.

August 10

Meditation: Picture the enduring flow of a river carving its way through a landscape, constantly adapting yet always moving forward. Let this continuous flow inspire persistence and adaptability in your own journey.

Affirmation: I move through life like a river, persistent and adaptable, carving my path through challenges and always flowing towards my goals.

Thought: Rivers, with their persistent forward movement, remind us of the importance of perseverance and the power of adaptability in navigating life's challenges.

Focus: Persistence and adaptability.

August 11

Meditation: Reflect on the warmth and vitality of the morning sun as it breaks the horizon, its rays spreading warmth and light. Let this daily renewal inspire a vibrant start to your day, filled with energy and optimism.

Affirmation: I welcome each day with the energy and optimism of the morning sun, allowing its vitality to invigorate my spirit and illuminate my path.

Thought: The morning sun, rising anew each day, teaches us the value of renewal and the potential of starting each day with renewed energy and a fresh outlook.

Focus: Renewal and vibrant starts.

August 12

Meditation: Imagine the gentle sway of trees in a soft breeze, their movements graceful and coordinated with the wind. Let this harmony with nature inspire balance and grace in your responses to life's fluctuations.

Affirmation: I sway gracefully with life's breezes, balanced and harmonious, adapting my movements to align with the rhythms of nature around me.

Thought: Trees swaying in the wind teach us the elegance of moving in harmony with the forces we encounter, embracing flexibility and balance.

Focus: Grace and balance in adaptation.

August 13

Meditation: Visualize the quiet majesty of a large boulder sitting steadfast in a bustling stream, water flowing around it. Let the boulder's unyielding presence amidst the flow inspire steadiness and resilience in your life.

Affirmation: I am as steadfast and resilient as a boulder in a stream, maintaining my calm and strength no matter the currents that swirl around me.

Thought: The boulder in the stream, unaffected by the constant flow, teaches us about resilience and the power of remaining steady in the face of life's relentless changes.

Focus: Steadiness and resilience.

August 14

Meditation: Consider the lifecycle of a leaf, from its budding in spring to its vibrant display in fall and eventual return to the earth. Let this natural cycle inspire acceptance of life's phases and the beauty in each.

Affirmation: I embrace each phase of my life, finding beauty and purpose in the natural progression from growth to maturity and renewal.

SACRED WISDOM – NATIVE AMERICAN MEDITATIONS, AFFIRMATIONS, AND REFLECTIONS

Thought: The leaf's lifecycle, marked by growth, vibrancy, and renewal, mirrors our own life phases, each holding its unique beauty and importance.

Focus: Embracing life's cycles and finding beauty in change.

August 15

Meditation: Picture the early morning mist hovering over a quiet meadow, slowly lifting as the sun rises. Let this gentle unveiling inspire clarity and the revealing of insights in your own understanding.

Affirmation: I welcome clarity as the mist of uncertainty lifts, revealing the bright meadow of understanding and insight beneath.

Thought: Morning mist, which obscures before it lifts to reveal the landscape, teaches us about the gradual clarity that comes with patience and the light of understanding.

Focus: Gaining clarity and understanding.

August 16

Meditation: Reflect on the sound of a crackling fire, the flames dancing and the wood hissing. Let this lively and warm environment inspire comfort and a spark of creativity in your engagements.

Affirmation: I nurture the spark of creativity within me, letting it dance and crackle like a fire, bringing warmth and innovation to my endeavors.

Thought: The crackling fire, with its warmth and dynamic flames, reminds us of the comfort of familiar sounds and the sparking of creativity that warmth can bring.

Focus: Comfort and creativity.

August 17

Meditation: Visualize a bird soaring high above the earth, effortless and free. Let this image inspire a sense of freedom and the pursuit of perspectives that rise above the mundane.

Affirmation: I soar above daily challenges, embracing the freedom to pursue higher perspectives and the peace that comes from a broadened view.

Thought: The soaring bird, free from earthly ties, teaches us about the liberation and clarity that come from elevating our perspective above the immediate.

Focus: Freedom and elevated perspectives.

August 18

Meditation: Imagine the rhythmic pulsing of the ocean's waves at night, consistent and soothing. Let the predictability and calm of this natural rhythm bring peace and stability to your mind.

Affirmation: I find peace in the rhythmic certainty of life's natural patterns, drawing calmness from the consistent pulse of the ocean's waves.

Thought: The ocean at night, with its rhythmic and soothing waves, reminds us of the comfort that can be found in life's reliable patterns and rhythms.

Focus: Peace and rhythmic stability.

August 19

Meditation: Consider the grounding presence of the Earth beneath your feet, solid and enduring. Let this connection to the Earth inspire a sense of grounding and a deep connection to your environment and community.

Affirmation: I am deeply grounded, connected to my environment and community with the solidity and endurance of the Earth itself.

Thought: The Earth, with its vast and enduring presence, teaches us the importance of grounding ourselves in our environment and relationships, finding stability and strength.

Focus: Grounding and connection to community.

August 20

Meditation: Picture the silent accumulation of snow on a winter's night, each flake contributing quietly to a blanket that transforms the landscape. Let this peaceful accumulation inspire patience and appreciation for gradual progress in your life.

Affirmation: I embrace the quiet and steady progress in my life, like snowflakes forming a transformative blanket, recognizing the power of small, cumulative actions.

Thought: The quiet snowfall, transforming landscapes silently and slowly, teaches us the beauty and impact of gradual, steady change.

Focus: Patience and the impact of gradual progress.

August 21

Meditation: Reflect on the vastness of a desert under the stars, its expansive and open landscape a canvas for the night sky. Let this openness inspire you to embrace vast possibilities and a broad perspective in your own life.

Affirmation: I open my heart and mind to vast possibilities, inspired by the expansive desert sky, ready to explore and embrace the wide array of opportunities before me.

Thought: The desert under the starlit sky, with its boundless space, reminds us of the infinite possibilities within and around us, urging us to explore broadly.

Focus: Embracing vast possibilities and exploring broadly.

August 22

Meditation: Imagine the growth of a vine, climbing and reaching towards the light, its path both determined and adaptable. Let this resilience and flexibility inspire your own paths toward personal goals.

Affirmation: I grow with determination and adaptability, like a vine reaching for the light, navigating my path with resilience and flexibility.

Thought: The climbing vine, with its persistent yet adaptable growth, teaches us the importance of resilience and flexibility in achieving our goals.

Focus: Resilience and adaptability in personal growth.

August 23

Meditation: Visualize the gentle flow of a creek, its water clear and constant, navigating around stones and branches effortlessly. Let this natural ease inspire a smooth and adaptable approach to life's obstacles.

Affirmation: I navigate life's obstacles with the ease of a flowing creek, moving smoothly around challenges and maintaining my path with clarity and grace.

Thought: The creek, with its effortless flow around obstacles, teaches us the value of adaptability and the importance of maintaining grace under pressure.

Focus: Graceful navigation of life's obstacles.

August 24

Meditation: Picture the first break of dawn on the horizon, the sky gradually lighting up with hues of orange and pink. Let this daily renewal inspire optimism and a fresh start in your endeavors.

Affirmation: I welcome each new day with optimism, inspired by the renewal of dawn, embracing each fresh start with energy and enthusiasm.

Thought: The break of dawn, with its promise of a new day, teaches us the power of renewal and the potential that each beginning holds, urging us to approach each day with renewed vigor.

Focus: Optimism and embracing fresh starts.

August 25

Meditation: Reflect on the protective and nurturing role of trees in a forest, offering shelter and sustenance to many forms of life. Let this sense of community and support inspire your own contributions to those around you.

Affirmation: I contribute to my community with the nurturing spirit of a forest, providing support and shelter, and fostering a sense of belonging and growth among those around me.

Thought: The forest, with its interconnected web of life, reminds us of the importance of community support, nurturing, and protection for collective well-being.

Focus: Nurturing community and providing support.

August 26

Meditation: Imagine the exhilarating sensation of standing atop a high peak, viewing the world from above. Let this elevated perspective inspire greater insight and a broader outlook on your personal and professional challenges.

SACRED WISDOM – NATIVE AMERICAN MEDITATIONS, AFFIRMATIONS, AND REFLECTIONS

Affirmation: I embrace an elevated perspective, viewing challenges and opportunities from a higher vantage point, which broadens my understanding and enhances my decision-making.

Thought: The view from a mountain peak, expansive and unobstructed, teaches us the value of seeing things from above, offering a clearer, broader perspective.

Focus: Gaining insight and a broader perspective.

August 27

Meditation: Picture the resilience of a wildflower growing in a crack in the sidewalk, its life force pushing through the concrete. Let this symbol of resilience and determination inspire your own growth, even in challenging conditions.

Affirmation: I channel the resilience of a wildflower, thriving in adversity and finding ways to grow, no matter the environment.

Thought: The wildflower, sprouting through concrete, teaches us that growth and beauty can emerge even in the most unlikely or challenging conditions.

Focus: Resilience and thriving in adversity.

August 28

Meditation: Reflect on the gentle fall of autumn leaves, each one following its own path to the ground. Let this natural release inspire you to let go of what no longer serves you, embracing change with grace.

Affirmation: I let go with the grace of falling leaves, releasing what no longer serves me, and welcoming the renewal this change brings.

Thought: The falling leaves of autumn, each gracefully descending, remind us of the beauty in release and the natural cycle of letting go and renewal.

Focus: Graceful release and embracing change.

August 29

Meditation: Visualize the steady accumulation of snow on a quiet winter night. Let the blanket of snow inspire a sense of peace and the quiet power of accumulation in achieving substantial impact.

SACRED WISDOM – NATIVE AMERICAN MEDITATIONS, AFFIRMATIONS, AND REFLECTIONS

Affirmation: I appreciate the quiet power of small, steady actions, knowing they accumulate to create significant impact, much like snow quietly covering the landscape.

Thought: Snowfall, silent and steady, accumulates into a transformative blanket, teaching us the power of small, consistent efforts in creating profound changes.

Focus: The power of accumulation and transformative impact.

August 30

Meditation: Imagine the peaceful flow of a river at dawn, its surface reflecting the soft morning light. Let this tranquil setting inspire calmness and reflection in your life, encouraging peaceful starts to your days.

Affirmation: I start each day with calmness and reflection, inspired by the tranquil flow of a river at dawn, embracing peace as I prepare for the day's challenges.

Thought: The calm river at dawn, reflective and serene, teaches us the value of starting our days in peace, setting a reflective and calm tone for whatever lies ahead.

Focus: Peaceful starts and reflective calmness.

August 31

Meditation: Consider the intricate beauty of a spider's web, each thread connected and essential. Let this interconnectedness inspire you to recognize and value the connections in your own life, seeing how each relationship supports and enhances the others.

Affirmation: I cherish and strengthen the connections in my life, understanding that, like a spider's web, each thread plays a crucial role in the overall strength and design.

Thought: The spider's web, complex and interconnected, shows us the beauty and strength of being connected, reminding us of the importance of our relationships and community ties.

Focus: Valuing and strengthening connections.

September 1

Meditation: Picture the first hint of sunrise coloring the horizon, the sky slowly brightening. Let this gradual illumination inspire optimism and the potential for renewal each day offers.

SACRED WISDOM – NATIVE ANERICAN MEDITATIONS, AFFIRMATIONS, AND REFLECTIONS

Affirmation: I greet each day with optimism, inspired by the sunrise's promise of a fresh start and the endless possibilities each new day holds.

Thought: The gradual brightening of the dawn teaches us that each day brings its own form of renewal and a chance to start afresh, filled with optimism and potential.

Focus: Optimism and daily renewal.

September 2

Meditation: Reflect on the calming sound of rain on a roof, rhythmic and soothing. Let this sound inspire relaxation and the embracing of life's simpler, comforting aspects.

Affirmation: I find comfort and relaxation in life's simple pleasures, like the soothing sound of rain, allowing these moments to refresh and calm my spirit.

Thought: The sound of rain, simple yet profoundly comforting, reminds us of the peace that can be found in life's quieter moments, encouraging us to embrace and cherish them.

Focus: Embracing simplicity and finding relaxation.

September 3

Meditation: Imagine the vast silence of a desert at night, the stillness so profound it seems to echo. Let this deep quietude inspire a sense of inner peace and the ability to find calm within yourself, even in solitude.

Affirmation: I embrace the profound peace of solitude, finding deep calm within myself, as serene as the desert at night.

Thought: The desert's vast silence teaches us the value of solitude and the profound peace that can come from embracing stillness within our own lives.

Focus: Inner peace and the power of solitude.

September 4

Meditation: Visualize the gentle lap of lake waters against the shore, a consistent and soothing touch. Let this gentle persistence inspire a steady and calming influence in your life and interactions.

SACRED WISDOM – NATIVE ANERICAN MEDITATIONS, AFFIRMATIONS, AND REFLECTIONS

Affirmation: I offer a steady and calming presence, like gentle lake waters, bringing consistency and peace to my surroundings and relationships.

Thought: The rhythmic lapping of lake waters against the shore teaches us about the soothing power of gentle, consistent presence in creating peace and stability.

Focus: Consistency and soothing influence.

September 5

Meditation: Picture the fiery colors of autumn leaves, their vibrant displays a final flourish before the winter. Let this natural spectacle inspire an appreciation for life's cyclical nature and the beauty in change.

Affirmation: I celebrate the beauty of change, embracing each cycle of life with the vibrancy and grace of autumn leaves.

Thought: Autumn leaves, with their spectacular colors, remind us that change is both inevitable and beautiful, a natural cycle to be embraced and celebrated.

Focus: Celebrating change and the beauty of life's cycles.

September 6

Meditation: Reflect on the quiet strength of a deer in the forest, moving with grace and alertness. Let this image inspire a balance of gentleness and resilience in your own approach to life's challenges.

Affirmation: I navigate life with the grace and strength of a forest deer, blending resilience with gentleness in my approach to challenges.

Thought: The deer's graceful yet resilient nature teaches us the power of gentle strength and the effectiveness of moving through life with alertness and grace.

Focus: Graceful resilience and balanced strength.

September 7

Meditation: Imagine the first frost of the season, its icy touch transforming leaves and grass into sparkling jewels. Let this transformation inspire a fresh perspective on the everyday, finding new beauty in the familiar.

Affirmation: I view the familiar with fresh eyes, allowing the transformative power of new perspectives to reveal hidden beauty, like frost on the landscape.

Thought: The first frost's ability to transform the mundane into the magical reminds us of the potential for beauty and wonder in everyday life, seen through fresh perspectives.

Focus: Fresh perspectives and finding beauty.

September 8

Meditation: Visualize the expansive view from a mountaintop, the world below offering a new scale and perspective. Let this broad view inspire expansive thinking and a broader understanding of your own life's landscape.

Affirmation: I adopt a broad perspective, viewing my life's challenges and opportunities from an elevated viewpoint, inspired by the expansive views from a mountaintop.

Thought: The view from a mountaintop, with its broad and sweeping vistas, teaches us the value of seeing things from above, gaining a clearer, more comprehensive understanding.

Focus: Expansive thinking and broad perspectives.

September 9

Meditation: Consider the steady growth of an oak tree, from acorn to mighty tree. Let this slow and powerful development inspire patience and faith in the gradual unfolding of your own potential.

Affirmation: I am patient and confident in my growth, trusting in the slow but steady process of unfolding my potential, like an oak tree from an acorn.

Thought: The oak tree's journey from acorn to towering strength reminds us of the power of gradual growth and the impressive results of patience and perseverance.

Focus: Patience and trust in personal growth.

September 10

Meditation: Picture the serene surface of a pond at dawn, undisturbed and reflecting the sky. Let this image of calmness and clarity inspire peace and reflection in your life.

Affirmation: I embrace the peace and clarity of a calm pond, reflecting on my life with tranquility and gaining clear insights from my surroundings.

Thought: The still pond at dawn, with its perfect reflections, teaches us the beauty of calmness and the clarity that comes with serenity, urging us to seek these qualities in our lives.

Focus: Peace, clarity, and serenity.

September 11

Meditation: Reflect on the cyclic journey of the moon, waxing and waning through its phases. Let this celestial rhythm inspire an understanding of life's natural cycles and the beauty in their continuity.

Affirmation: I appreciate and align with the natural cycles of life, finding beauty and meaning in each phase, just as the moon gracefully transitions through its cycles.

Thought: The moon's phases, with their reliable pattern, remind us of the inevitable cycles in our own lives, each bringing its own lessons and beauty.

Focus: Appreciation of life's natural cycles.

September 12

Meditation: Imagine the fierce beauty of a lightning storm, its raw power both awe-inspiring and transformative. Let this display of nature's force inspire boldness and a dynamic approach to your challenges.

Affirmation: I harness the boldness and energy of a lightning storm, approaching life's challenges with dynamic force and transformative power.

Thought: Lightning, with its sudden and powerful impact, teaches us about the potency of taking decisive, bold action, and the transformation that can follow.

Focus: Boldness and dynamic transformation.

September 13

Meditation: Visualize the intricate weaving of a bird's nest, each strand purposefully placed for strength and shelter. Let this careful craftsmanship inspire diligence and attention to detail in your own endeavors.

SACRED WISDOM – NATIVE ANERICAN MEDITATIONS, AFFIRMATIONS, AND REFLECTIONS

Affirmation: I approach my tasks with the diligence and precision of a bird building its nest, weaving each aspect of my work with care and intention.

Thought: The bird's nest, crafted with meticulous care, teaches us the value of attention to detail and the strength that comes from thoughtful, purposeful work.

Focus: Diligence and meticulous craftsmanship.

September 14

Meditation: Consider the soothing rhythm of a gentle rain, its steady pattern nurturing the earth. Let this soothing regularity bring a sense of calm and renewal to your spirit.

Affirmation: I find renewal and calm in life's steady rhythms, like the soothing rain that nurtures the earth, refreshing my spirit and outlook.

Thought: Gentle rain, with its rhythmic and nurturing touch, reminds us of the renewing power of nature's rhythms, encouraging us to embrace and find solace in them.

Focus: Renewal and calm through nature's rhythms.

September 15

Meditation: Picture the first buds of spring emerging from the earth, their appearance signaling renewal and new growth. Let this natural reawakening inspire a sense of hope and new beginnings in your life.

Affirmation: I embrace new beginnings with the hope and freshness of spring buds, allowing the spirit of renewal to invigorate my life and aspirations.

Thought: Spring buds, pushing through the soil to bloom, symbolize the perennial hope and renewal in nature, urging us to adopt a similar freshness and optimism.

Focus: Hope and new beginnings.

September 16

Meditation: Reflect on the warmth and light of a campfire gathering, its glow uniting those around it. Let this sense of community and warmth inspire connections and shared experiences in your own life.

Affirmation: I cultivate warmth and connection in my relationships, drawing together a community of support and shared joy, like a campfire brings together those around it.

Thought: The campfire, with its inviting warmth and communal light, teaches us the value of gathering together, sharing experiences, and strengthening bonds.

Focus: Building community and sharing warmth.

September 17

Meditation: Imagine the steadfast presence of an ancient oak tree, witnessing centuries of history, strong and dignified. Let this image of enduring strength and wisdom inspire steadiness and depth in your character.

Affirmation: I draw upon the deep wisdom and strength of the ancient oak, embodying its steadiness and dignity in facing life's challenges and changes.

Thought: The ancient oak, enduring through time, teaches us about resilience, the wisdom gained from longevity, and the quiet dignity in steadfastness.

Focus: Enduring strength and wisdom.

September 18

Meditation: Visualize a river cutting through a canyon, its waters shaping the landscape over millennia. Let this powerful natural process inspire perseverance and the transformative impact of consistent effort.

Affirmation: I channel the transformative power of persistence, like a river shaping a canyon, knowing that steady efforts yield profound results over time.

Thought: The river's relentless flow, carving through rock, teaches us the immense power of persistence and the lasting impact of continual effort.

Focus: Perseverance and transformative impact.

September 19

SACRED WISDOM – NATIVE AMERICAN MEDITATIONS, AFFIRMATIONS, AND REFLECTIONS

Meditation: Reflect on the soothing silence of a snowy landscape, the world muffled and serene under a blanket of snow. Let this quietude inspire inner peace and a refreshing pause in your busy life.

Affirmation: I embrace the serene silence of a snowy day, finding peace and a moment to pause, allowing myself to rejuvenate amidst life's busyness.

Thought: The quiet of a snowy landscape, with its capacity to pause the usual sounds of life, reminds us of the peace found in stillness and the refreshing nature of silence.

Focus: Inner peace and the value of quiet.

September 20

Meditation: Picture the dynamic and vibrant colors of a sunset, each hue blending into the next. Let this daily spectacle of color inspire creativity and a vibrant approach to your personal and professional projects.

Affirmation: I infuse my actions with the vibrant creativity of a sunset, blending ideas and inspirations like the colors in the sky, crafting a spectacular end to each day.

Thought: The sunset, with its breathtaking blend of colors, teaches us about the beauty of combining different elements creatively, encouraging vibrant and innovative expressions.

Focus: Creativity and vibrant expressions.

September 21

Meditation: Imagine the resilience of wildlife preparing for winter, each species adapting in its own way to survive the colder months. Let this natural preparedness inspire thoughtful planning and resilience in your own endeavors.

Affirmation: I prepare for future challenges with the resilience of nature, thoughtfully planning and adapting to ensure sustainability and success.

Thought: The preparedness of wildlife for winter, each adaptation crucial for survival, teaches us the importance of foresight and the resilience in well-planned adaptations.

Focus: Thoughtful planning and resilience.

September 22

SACRED WISDOM – NATIVE ANERICAN MEDITATIONS, AFFIRMATIONS, AND REFLECTIONS

Meditation: Visualize the calm expanse of the night sky, clear and studded with stars. Let this vast and peaceful space inspire a sense of calm and the realization that the universe is vast, and our troubles are small in comparison.

Affirmation: I find calmness and perspective under the vast night sky, reminded that my troubles, while significant, are small within the expanse of the universe.

Thought: The expansive night sky, with its endless stars, teaches us about perspective, reminding us of our place in the universe and the relative scale of our concerns.

Focus: Calm perspective and universal scale.

September 23

Meditation: Reflect on the gentle but persistent touch of wind shaping a landscape, its invisible force powerful over time. Let this subtle influence inspire you to recognize the power of gentle, consistent efforts in shaping your life and goals.

Affirmation: I embrace the power of gentle persistence, like the wind shaping the landscape, knowing that steady, soft efforts can achieve significant change.

Thought: The wind, though soft and often unnoticed, has the power to alter landscapes over time, teaching us the effectiveness of persistence and the impact of gentle forces.

Focus: Gentle persistence and the power of subtlety.

September 24

Meditation: Imagine the expansive view of the ocean, stretching to the horizon where the sea meets the sky. Let this boundless view inspire openness and the removal of limitations in your thinking.

Affirmation: I embrace the boundlessness of the ocean, expanding my horizons and removing limitations from my thinking, inspired by the vast sea that meets the sky.

Thought: The ocean's expansive view teaches us about the limitless potential of our minds when we remove barriers and open ourselves to broader horizons.

Focus: Expansiveness and openness in thinking.

September 25

Meditation: Reflect on the intricate pattern of an autumn leaf, its veins like a roadmap of life's journey. Let this natural artistry inspire appreciation for life's complexities and the beauty found in every detail.

Affirmation: I celebrate the complexity and detail in life, finding beauty in the intricate patterns that resemble the veins of an autumn leaf, each line telling a story of growth and change.

Thought: Autumn leaves, with their detailed patterns, remind us that life's complexities are interwoven with beauty, and each detail adds to our understanding and appreciation of the whole.

Focus: Appreciation of complexity and detail.

September 26

Meditation: Picture the steady ascent of a hot air balloon at sunrise, rising quietly above the waking world. Let this peaceful and steady rise inspire confidence and a smooth approach to achieving your goals.

Affirmation: I ascend towards my goals steadily and peacefully, like a hot air balloon at sunrise, rising above challenges with grace and confidence.

Thought: The hot air balloon's ascent at sunrise, peaceful and steady, teaches us the value of maintaining composure and confidence as we rise above everyday challenges.

Focus: Steady ascent and graceful achievement.

September 27

Meditation: Imagine the warmth and crackle of a campfire, drawing people together in its glow. Let this sense of community and shared warmth inspire connection and the fostering of relationships in your life.

Affirmation: I nurture connections and foster warmth in my relationships, drawing together a community of support and shared joy, much like a campfire brings people together.

Thought: The campfire, with its inviting warmth and communal glow, teaches us about the importance of coming together, sharing our stories, and building strong bonds.

Focus: Building community and nurturing relationships.

September 28

Meditation: Reflect on the silent endurance of mountains, standing firm for millennia. Let this enduring strength inspire resilience and a long-term perspective in your personal and professional endeavors.

Affirmation: I embody the enduring strength of mountains, standing resilient through time, maintaining a long-term perspective that guides my decisions and actions.

Thought: Mountains, with their ancient and steadfast presence, teach us resilience and the power of a long-term perspective in facing life's transient challenges.

Focus: Resilience and long-term perspective.

September 29

Meditation: Visualize the delicate dance of snowflakes falling in a winter storm, each unique and beautiful. Let this dance of uniqueness inspire creativity and the celebration of individuality in your interactions and self-expression.

Affirmation: I celebrate uniqueness and express creativity, inspired by the delicate dance of snowflakes, each unique and contributing its beauty to the whole.

Thought: Snowflakes, unique in their structure and beautiful in their descent, remind us of the importance of celebrating individuality and the creative expression of each person.

Focus: Creativity and celebration of individuality.

September 30

Meditation: Picture the slow and majestic flow of a glacier, moving imperceptibly but with immense force. Let this powerful and deliberate motion inspire determination and unstoppable progress towards your aspirations.

Affirmation: I move towards my aspirations with the unstoppable force of a glacier, my progress deliberate and powerful, shaping the landscape of my life over time.

Thought: Glaciers, with their slow but powerful movement, teach us the effectiveness of steady, determined progress in achieving significant impact and long-term change.

Focus: Determination and unstoppable progress.

October 1

SACRED WISDOM – NATIVE ANERICAN MEDITATIONS, AFFIRMATIONS, AND REFLECTIONS

Meditation: Imagine the vibrant and varied colors of fall foliage, each leaf a masterpiece of change and transformation. Let this colorful display inspire acceptance of change and an appreciation for life's cycles.

Affirmation: I embrace the vibrant changes in my life, seeing the beauty in transformation, much like the fall foliage that turns every ending into a spectacular display.

Thought: The fall foliage, with its vibrant colors, teaches us that change is not only inevitable but can also be beautiful, enriching our lives with new textures and hues.

Focus: Acceptance of change and appreciation of life's beauty.

October 2

Meditation: Reflect on the gentle descent of a feather floating down from the sky, its journey smooth and unhurried. Let this image inspire ease and grace in handling life's ups and downs.

Affirmation: I handle life's changes with the grace and ease of a feather floating down, smoothly navigating the currents of change with calm and poise.

Thought: A feather's descent, graceful and serene, reminds us that we too can approach life's fluctuations with tranquility, turning potential descents into graceful journeys.

Focus: Grace and ease in transitions.

October 3

Meditation: Picture the steady growth of a sequoia, each year adding layers of strength and height. Let this image of enduring and steady growth inspire long-term vision and persistence in your personal development.

Affirmation: I cultivate my growth with the persistence and endurance of a sequoia, building strength and stature over time, with a vision for the long-term journey.

Thought: The sequoia, towering and ancient, teaches us the virtues of steady growth and the impressive results of persistence and long-term vision.

Focus: Long-term growth and persistence.

October 4

SACRED WISDOM – NATIVE ANERICAN MEDITATIONS, AFFIRMATIONS, AND REFLECTIONS

Meditation: Imagine the rhythmic pattern of raindrops during a shower, each contributing to the nourishment of the earth. Let this nurturing rhythm inspire you to contribute positively and consistently to your surroundings.

Affirmation: I contribute to my environment with the consistency and nourishment of rain, each action adding value and fostering growth around me.

Thought: Rain, essential and rhythmic, provides life-giving nourishment, reminding us that our consistent contributions can similarly sustain and enrich our communities.

Focus: Consistent contribution and nurturing.

October 5

Meditation: Visualize the warmth of a morning sun piercing through a morning mist, clearing it away with its brightness. Let this clearing inspire clarity and illumination in your thoughts and decisions.

Affirmation: I embrace clarity and illumination, like the morning sun disperses the mist, clearing the way for enlightened thoughts and decisive actions.

Thought: The morning sun, with its power to dispel the mist, teaches us the value of clarity and the transformative impact of bringing light to our uncertainties.

Focus: Clarity and illumination.

October 6

Meditation: Reflect on the protective circle of a ring of stones around a campfire, keeping the fire contained and safe. Let this circle inspire you to establish boundaries that protect and nurture your personal space and growth.

Affirmation: I establish and maintain healthy boundaries, like a circle of stones around a fire, protecting my energy and fostering a safe space for growth.

Thought: The circle of stones around a campfire, a safeguard and boundary, teaches us the importance of setting limits that protect and enhance our personal well-being.

Focus: Establishing protective boundaries.

October 7

SACRED WISDOM – NATIVE ANERICAN MEDITATIONS, AFFIRMATIONS, AND REFLECTIONS

Meditation: Picture the quiet resilience of a cactus in the desert, thriving in an environment of extreme conditions. Let this resilience inspire you to thrive despite challenges, using your inner strength to adapt and succeed.

Affirmation: I thrive in all conditions, drawing on the resilience of a desert cactus, using my inner strength and adaptability to overcome and prosper.

Thought: The cactus, resilient and adaptive, demonstrates how to thrive in challenging environments, encouraging us to find strength and thrive in our own difficult situations.

Focus: Resilience and thriving in adversity.

October 8

Meditation: Visualize yourself standing on the edge of a canyon, feeling the vastness of the world around you. Allow this image to inspire you to embrace the unknown with courage and openness.

Affirmation: I embrace the unknown with courage and openness, knowing that each step forward is a step into new possibilities and growth.

Thought: The canyon's vastness reminds us of the endless opportunities that await us when we step outside of our comfort zone and into the unknown.

Focus: Embracing the unknown with courage and openness.

October 9

Meditation: Picture the gentle flutter of a butterfly's wings, each movement a symbol of transformation and change. Let this image inspire you to welcome change in your life with grace and acceptance.

Affirmation: I welcome change in my life with grace and acceptance, knowing that each transformation brings me closer to my true self.

Thought: The butterfly's transformation from caterpillar to butterfly teaches us about the beauty and necessity of change in our own lives.

Focus: Welcoming change with grace and acceptance.

October 10

Meditation: Imagine yourself sitting around a campfire, the warmth and light enveloping you. Let this image inspire you to find comfort and solace in moments of darkness.

Affirmation: I find comfort and solace in moments of darkness, like the warmth and light of a campfire, knowing that light always follows the darkest of nights.

Thought: The campfire's warmth and light remind us that even in our darkest moments, there is always a glimmer of hope and light to guide us.

Focus: Finding comfort and solace in moments of darkness.

October 11

Meditation: Visualize the quiet strength of a tree, its roots grounding it firmly in the earth. Allow this image to inspire you to find stability and strength within yourself.

Affirmation: I am grounded and strong, like the tree with deep roots, finding stability and strength in the midst of life's storms.

Thought: The tree's deep roots teach us about the importance of finding stability and strength within ourselves, even in the face of adversity.

Focus: Finding stability and strength within.

October 12

Meditation: Picture the gentle flow of a river, its waters carving a path through the landscape. Let this image inspire you to go with the flow of life, trusting in the journey.

Affirmation: I go with the flow of life, like a river carving its path, trusting in the journey and knowing that each twist and turn has purpose.

Thought: The river's steady flow teaches us about the importance of trusting in the journey of life, embracing its twists and turns with grace and acceptance.

Focus: Going with the flow and trusting in the journey.

October 13

SACRED WISDOM – NATIVE AMERICAN MEDITATIONS, AFFIRMATIONS, AND REFLECTIONS

Meditation: Reflect on the quiet resilience of a flower blooming in the desert, its beauty a testament to strength and perseverance. Let this image inspire you to bloom despite adversity.

Affirmation: I bloom despite adversity, like a flower in the desert, my beauty and strength shining through challenges and hardships.

Thought: The flower blooming in the desert teaches us about the power of resilience and perseverance, reminding us that beauty can thrive in the most unlikely of places.

Focus: Blooming despite adversity.

October 14

Meditation: Imagine the vast expanse of the night sky, filled with stars that have guided travelers for millennia. Let this image inspire you to trust in your own inner guidance.

Affirmation: I trust in my own inner guidance, like the stars that have guided travelers for millennia, knowing that I am guided towards my true path.

Thought: The stars in the night sky, guiding travelers, teach us about the importance of trusting in our own inner guidance and intuition.

Focus: Trusting in inner guidance.

October 15

Meditation: Imagine the quiet strength of a boulder in a river, the water flowing around it with persistence. Let this image inspire you to remain steadfast and resilient in the face of life's currents.

Affirmation: I am as steadfast as a boulder in the river, standing strong against life's currents, embracing resilience and unwavering strength.

Thought: The boulder in the river, unmoved by the current, teaches us the value of remaining steadfast and resilient in the face of life's challenges, standing strong against adversity.

Focus: Steadfastness and resilience.

October 16

SACRED WISDOM – NATIVE ANERICAN MEDITATIONS, AFFIRMATIONS, AND REFLECTIONS

Meditation: Reflect on the silent communication of a flock of birds in flight, each movement coordinated and purposeful. Let this natural synchrony inspire harmony and cooperation in your interactions.

Affirmation: I foster harmony and cooperation in my interactions, like a flock of birds in flight, moving with synchrony and purpose towards shared goals.

Thought: The synchronized flight of birds teaches us about the power of cooperation and harmony, reminding us of the strength found in unity and shared purpose.

Focus: Harmony and cooperation in interactions.

October 17

Meditation: Visualize the intricate web of a spider, each thread essential to its structure. Let this image inspire you to recognize the interconnectedness of all things and the importance of your actions.

Affirmation: I acknowledge my interconnectedness with all things, like the threads of a spider's web, recognizing that my actions have far-reaching effects on the world around me.

Thought: The spider's web, intricately woven and interconnected, teaches us about the interdependence of all life and the impact of our actions on the greater web of existence.

Focus: Interconnectedness and mindful actions.

October 18

Meditation: Picture the gentle guidance of moonlight on a dark night, illuminating the path ahead. Let this image inspire you to trust your intuition and inner guidance in navigating life's journey.

Affirmation: I trust my intuition and inner guidance, like the moonlight that illuminates my path, knowing that I am guided towards the right direction in life.

Thought: The moonlight's gentle glow, guiding us through darkness, teaches us the importance of trusting our inner guidance and intuition to lead us towards the light.

Focus: Trusting intuition and inner guidance.

SACRED WISDOM – NATIVE ANERICAN MEDITATIONS, AFFIRMATIONS, AND REFLECTIONS

October 19

Meditation: Imagine the patience of a spider spinning its web, each movement deliberate and precise. Let this image inspire you to approach your tasks with patience and attention to detail.

Affirmation: I approach my tasks with patience and attention to detail, like a spider spinning its web, knowing that each deliberate action contributes to the whole.

Thought: The spider's patient web-spinning teaches us about the value of meticulousness and attention to detail, reminding us that great things are achieved one step at a time.

Focus: Patience and attention to detail.

October 20

Meditation: Reflect on the deep roots of a tree, anchoring it firmly in the earth. Let this image inspire you to cultivate deep roots of your own, grounding you in your values and beliefs.

Affirmation: I cultivate deep roots in my values and beliefs, like a tree firmly anchored in the earth, grounding me and providing strength in times of challenge.

Thought: The tree's deep roots, anchoring it in the earth, teach us about the importance of grounding ourselves in our values and beliefs, providing stability and strength.

Focus: Cultivating deep roots in values and beliefs.

October 21

Meditation: Picture the gentle flow of a stream, its waters meandering peacefully through the landscape. Let this image inspire you to go with the flow of life, embracing its natural course.

Affirmation: I go with the flow of life, like a stream meandering through the landscape, adapting and flowing gracefully with the currents of change.

Thought: The stream's gentle flow teaches us the value of going with the flow, adapting to change with grace and embracing the natural course of life's journey.

Focus: Going with the flow and embracing change.

SACRED WISDOM – NATIVE ANERICAN MEDITATIONS, AFFIRMATIONS, AND REFLECTIONS

October 22

Meditation: Imagine the persistent growth of a vine, slowly but steadily climbing towards the sun. Let this image inspire you to pursue your goals with determination and perseverance.

Affirmation: I pursue my goals with determination and perseverance, like a vine climbing towards the sun, knowing that steady progress leads to great heights.

Thought: The vine's steady climb teaches us about the power of perseverance and the rewards that come from consistent effort towards our aspirations.

Focus: Determination and perseverance in pursuing goals.

October 23

Meditation: Reflect on the gentle sway of grass in the wind, each blade bending but not breaking. Let this image inspire flexibility and resilience in the face of life's challenges.

Affirmation: I am flexible and resilient, like the grass bending in the wind, adapting to life's challenges without losing my strength or resolve.

Thought: The grass's ability to bend without breaking teaches us about the value of flexibility and resilience in adapting to life's ever-changing circumstances.

Focus: Flexibility and resilience in facing challenges.

October 24

Meditation: Visualize the intricate patterns of frost on a window, each formation unique and beautiful. Let this natural artistry inspire appreciation for the beauty found in impermanence.

Affirmation: I appreciate the beauty of impermanence, like frost patterns on a window, recognizing the fleeting yet exquisite nature of life's moments.

Thought: Frost patterns, temporary and intricate, teach us about the beauty found in transient experiences, reminding us to cherish each moment as it comes.

Focus: Appreciating beauty in impermanence.

SACRED WISDOM – NATIVE AMERICAN MEDITATIONS, AFFIRMATIONS, AND REFLECTIONS

October 25

Meditation: Picture the steady glow of a lighthouse on a stormy night, guiding ships to safety. Let this image inspire you to be a beacon of hope and guidance for others in difficult times.

Affirmation: I am a beacon of hope and guidance for others, like a lighthouse guiding ships to safety, offering light and reassurance in times of darkness.

Thought: The lighthouse's steady glow teaches us about the importance of being a source of light and guidance for others, offering hope and direction in their journeys.

Focus: Being a beacon of hope and guidance.

October 26

Meditation: Imagine the gentle touch of rain on the earth, nourishing and renewing life. Let this image inspire you to nurture and care for yourself, allowing for growth and renewal.

Affirmation: I nurture and care for myself, like the gentle rain nourishing the earth, allowing for growth and renewal in my mind, body, and spirit.

Thought: The rain's nurturing touch teaches us the importance of self-care and nourishment, reminding us to take time to nurture our own well-being.

Focus: Self-care and nurturing for growth.

October 27

Meditation: Reflect on the intricate design of a spider's web, each thread essential to its strength. Let this image inspire you to recognize the interconnectedness of all things and the impact of your actions.

Affirmation: I acknowledge my interconnectedness with all things, like the threads of a spider's web, recognizing that my actions have far-reaching effects on the world around me.

Thought: The spider's web, intricately woven and interconnected, teaches us about the interdependence of all life and the importance of mindful actions.

Focus: Interconnectedness and mindful actions.

SACRED WISDOM – NATIVE ANERICAN MEDITATIONS, AFFIRMATIONS, AND REFLECTIONS

October 28

Meditation: Visualize the quiet strength of a mountain, standing tall and unyielding. Let this image inspire you to embody resilience and steadfastness in the face of challenges.

Affirmation: I am as strong as a mountain, standing tall and unyielding in the face of challenges, embodying resilience and steadfastness in all aspects of my life.

Thought: The mountain's quiet strength teaches us about resilience and the power of standing firm in the face of adversity, reminding us of our own inner strength.

Focus: Resilience and steadfastness in challenges.

October 29

Meditation: Imagine the gentle dance of flames in a campfire, each flicker mesmerizing and unique. Let this image inspire you to embrace your own unique qualities and talents.

Affirmation: I embrace my uniqueness, like the dance of flames in a campfire, recognizing that my individuality is a source of strength and beauty.

Thought: The dance of flames in a campfire, each flicker different from the next, teaches us about the beauty and strength found in embracing our own unique qualities.

Focus: Embracing uniqueness and individuality.

October 30

Meditation: Picture the graceful flight of a butterfly, its wings carrying it effortlessly through the air. Let this image inspire you to move through life with grace and lightness.

Affirmation: I move through life with grace and lightness, like a butterfly fluttering through the air, embracing the beauty and joy of each moment.

Thought: The butterfly's graceful flight teaches us about the beauty of moving through life with grace and lightness, reminding us to savor each moment.

Focus: Grace and lightness in movement.

SACRED WISDOM – NATIVE ANERICAN MEDITATIONS, AFFIRMATIONS, AND REFLECTIONS

October 31

Meditation: Reflect on the quiet wisdom of an elder, their words carrying the weight of experience. Let this image inspire you to seek wisdom and guidance from those who have walked before you.

Affirmation: I seek wisdom from those who have walked before me, honoring the experience and guidance of elders, knowing that their words carry valuable insights.

Thought: The wisdom of an elder, gained through a lifetime of experiences, teaches us the value of seeking guidance and learning from those who have lived longer.

Focus: Seeking wisdom and guidance from elders.

November 1

Meditation: Visualize the steady growth of a tree, each year adding new rings of strength and resilience. Let this image inspire you to grow steadily in your own life, adding layers of wisdom and experience.

Affirmation: I grow steadily in my life, like a tree adding new rings of strength and resilience each year, knowing that my experiences enrich and strengthen me.

Thought: The tree's steady growth teaches us about the value of growing steadily in our own lives, adding layers of wisdom and resilience with each passing year.

Focus: Steady growth and adding layers of wisdom.

November 2

Meditation: Imagine the quiet power of a sunrise, its light gradually illuminating the world. Let this image inspire you to approach new beginnings with a sense of hope and optimism.

Affirmation: I embrace new beginnings with hope and optimism, like the sunrise gradually illuminating the world, knowing that each day brings new possibilities.

Thought: The sunrise, with its quiet power, teaches us about the beauty and potential found in new beginnings, reminding us to approach them with a sense of hope and optimism.

Focus: Hope and optimism in new beginnings.

SACRED WISDOM – NATIVE AMERICAN MEDITATIONS, AFFIRMATIONS, AND REFLECTIONS

November 3

Meditation: Picture the intricate patterns of sand in a desert, shaped by the wind into unique formations. Let this image inspire you to see beauty in change and impermanence.

Affirmation: I see beauty in change and impermanence, like the intricate patterns of sand in a desert, knowing that each moment is fleeting yet beautiful in its own way.

Thought: The patterns of sand in a desert, shaped by the wind, teach us about the beauty found in impermanence and the ever-changing nature of life.

Focus: Seeing beauty in change and impermanence.

November 4

Meditation: Reflect on the quiet strength of a turtle, carrying its home on its back wherever it goes. Let this image inspire you to find strength and stability within yourself.

Affirmation: I carry my strength and stability within me, like a turtle carrying its home on its back, knowing that I am grounded and secure wherever I go.

Thought: The turtle's quiet strength teaches us about finding stability and security within ourselves, carrying our strength with us wherever life takes us.

Focus: Finding strength and stability within.

November 5

Meditation: Imagine the gentle rustle of leaves in a forest, each tree swaying in harmony with the breeze. Let this image inspire you to find harmony and balance in your own life.

Affirmation: I find harmony and balance in my life, like the trees swaying in the forest, moving in harmony with the rhythms of life.

Thought: The forest's harmony, with each tree swaying in rhythm, teaches us about the importance of finding balance and moving in sync with the world around us.

Focus: Finding harmony and balance in life.

SACRED WISDOM – NATIVE AMERICAN MEDITATIONS, AFFIRMATIONS, AND REFLECTIONS

November 6

Meditation: Picture the intricate dance of a raindrop on a leaf, each movement deliberate and graceful. Let this image inspire you to move through life with intention and grace.

Affirmation: I move through life with intention and grace, like a raindrop dancing on a leaf, each movement deliberate and meaningful.

Thought: The raindrop's dance on a leaf teaches us about the beauty and power of moving through life with intention and grace, embracing each moment fully.

Focus: Moving with intention and grace.

November 7

Meditation: Visualize the silent strength of a rock formation, standing tall against the elements. Let this image inspire you to stand firm in your beliefs and values.

Affirmation: I stand firm in my beliefs and values, like a rock formation standing tall against the elements, unwavering in my convictions.

Thought: The rock formation's silent strength teaches us about the importance of standing firm in our beliefs and values, even in the face of adversity.

Focus: Standing firm in beliefs and values.

November 8

Meditation: Imagine the gentle touch of a breeze on your skin, its presence fleeting yet soothing. Let this image inspire you to appreciate life's fleeting moments of beauty.

Affirmation: I appreciate life's fleeting moments of beauty, like the gentle touch of a breeze on my skin, knowing that each moment is precious and fleeting.

Thought: The breeze's fleeting touch teaches us about the beauty found in transient experiences, reminding us to cherish each moment as it comes.

Focus: Appreciating life's fleeting moments.

SACRED WISDOM – NATIVE ANERICAN MEDITATIONS, AFFIRMATIONS, AND REFLECTIONS

November 9

Meditation: Reflect on the quiet resilience of a flower blooming in the desert, its beauty a testament to strength and perseverance. Let this image inspire you to bloom despite adversity.

Affirmation: I bloom despite adversity, like a flower in the desert, my beauty and strength shining through challenges and hardships.

Thought: The flower blooming in the desert teaches us about the power of resilience and perseverance, reminding us that beauty can thrive in the most unlikely of places.

Focus: Blooming despite adversity.

November 10

Meditation: Picture the vast expanse of the night sky, filled with stars that have guided travelers for millennia. Let this image inspire you to trust in your own inner guidance.

Affirmation: I trust in my own inner guidance, like the stars that have guided travelers for millennia, knowing that I am guided towards my true path.

Thought: The stars in the night sky, guiding travelers, teach us about the importance of trusting in our own inner guidance and intuition.

Focus: Trusting in inner guidance.

November 11

Meditation: Imagine the steady flow of a river, its waters carving a path through the landscape. Let this image inspire you to go with the flow of life, trusting in the journey.

Affirmation: I go with the flow of life, like a river carving its path, trusting in the journey and knowing that each twist and turn has purpose.

Thought: The river's steady flow teaches us about the importance of trusting in the journey of life, embracing its twists and turns with grace and acceptance.

Focus: Going with the flow and trusting in the journey.

SACRED WISDOM – NATIVE AMERICAN MEDITATIONS, AFFIRMATIONS, AND REFLECTIONS

November 12

Meditation: Imagine the quiet strength of a mountain, standing tall and majestic. Let this image inspire you to embody strength and resilience in the face of challenges.

Affirmation: I embody strength and resilience, like a mountain standing tall and unwavering, facing challenges with grace and determination.

Thought: The mountain's quiet strength teaches us about the power of standing firm in the face of adversity, reminding us of our own inner strength.

Focus: Embodying strength and resilience.

November 13

Meditation: Picture the gentle rustle of leaves in a breeze, each movement a dance of life. Let this image inspire you to embrace the ever-changing nature of existence.

Affirmation: I embrace the ever-changing nature of existence, like leaves dancing in the breeze, moving with grace and acceptance.

Thought: The leaves' dance in the breeze teaches us about the beauty and inevitability of change, reminding us to embrace each moment as it comes.

Focus: Embracing the ever-changing nature of existence.

November 14

Meditation: Visualize the intricate patterns of a spider's web, each thread essential to its strength. Let this image inspire you to recognize the interconnectedness of all life.

Affirmation: I acknowledge my interconnectedness with all life, like the threads of a spider's web, knowing that my actions affect the greater whole.

Thought: The spider's web, intricately woven and interconnected, teaches us about the interdependence of all life and the impact of our actions on the world around us.

Focus: Recognizing the interconnectedness of all life.

SACRED WISDOM – NATIVE ANERICAN MEDITATIONS, AFFIRMATIONS, AND REFLECTIONS

November 15

Meditation: Imagine the quiet wisdom of an elder, their words carrying the weight of experience. Let this image inspire you to seek guidance from those who have walked before you.

Affirmation: I seek guidance from elders and wise individuals, honoring their experience and wisdom, knowing that their insights are valuable.

Thought: The wisdom of an elder, gained through a lifetime of experiences, teaches us the value of seeking guidance and learning from those who have lived longer.

Focus: Seeking wisdom from elders and wise individuals.

November 16

Meditation: Reflect on the intricate dance of a raindrop on a window, each movement a reflection of its journey. Let this image inspire you to see the beauty in simple moments.

Affirmation: I appreciate the beauty in simple moments, like the dance of a raindrop on a window, recognizing the magic in everyday experiences.

Thought: The raindrop's dance on a window teaches us about the beauty found in simple moments, reminding us to cherish the magic of everyday life.

Focus: Seeing the beauty in simple moments.

November 17

Meditation: Picture the gentle glow of a lantern in the darkness, its light guiding the way. Let this image inspire you to be a light for others in times of need.

Affirmation: I am a light for others in times of darkness, like a lantern guiding the way, offering warmth and guidance.

Thought: The lantern's gentle glow in the darkness teaches us about the importance of being a source of light and warmth for others, especially in their times of need.

Focus: Being a light for others in times of darkness.

SACRED WISDOM – NATIVE ANERICAN MEDITATIONS, AFFIRMATIONS, AND REFLECTIONS

November 18

Meditation: Imagine the vibrant colors of a sunset, painting the sky with beauty. Let this image inspire you to find beauty in endings and new beginnings.

Affirmation: I find beauty in endings and new beginnings, like the vibrant colors of a sunset, embracing the beauty of change.

Thought: The sunset's vibrant colors teach us about the beauty found in endings and new beginnings, reminding us that change can be a source of beauty and growth.

Focus: Finding beauty in endings and new beginnings.

November 19

Meditation: Visualize the quiet strength of a tree, its roots grounding it firmly in the earth. Let this image inspire you to find grounding and stability in your own life.

Affirmation: I am grounded and stable, like a tree with deep roots, finding strength and stability in the midst of life's challenges.

Thought: The tree's deep roots, anchoring it in the earth, teach us about the importance of finding grounding and stability in our own lives.

Focus: Finding grounding and stability.

November 20

Meditation: Picture the gentle flow of a river, its waters carving a path through the landscape. Let this image inspire you to go with the flow of life, trusting in the journey.

Affirmation: I go with the flow of life, like a river carving its path, trusting in the journey and knowing that each twist and turn has purpose.

Thought: The river's steady flow teaches us about the importance of trusting in the journey of life, embracing its twists and turns with grace and acceptance.

Focus: Going with the flow and trusting in the journey.

November 21

Meditation: Imagine the intricate patterns of sand in a desert, shaped by the wind into unique formations. Let this image inspire you to see beauty in change and impermanence.

Affirmation: I see beauty in change and impermanence, like the intricate patterns of sand in a desert, knowing that each moment is fleeting yet beautiful in its own way.

Thought: The patterns of sand in a desert, shaped by the wind, teach us about the beauty found in impermanence and the ever-changing nature of life.

Focus: Seeing beauty in change and impermanence.

November 22

Meditation: Reflect on the quiet resilience of a flower blooming in the desert, its beauty a testament to strength and perseverance. Let this image inspire you to bloom despite adversity.

Affirmation: I bloom despite adversity, like a flower in the desert, my beauty and strength shining through challenges and hardships.

Thought: The flower blooming in the desert teaches us about the power of resilience and perseverance, reminding us that beauty can thrive in the most unlikely of places.

Focus: Blooming despite adversity.

November 23

Meditation: Picture the vast expanse of the night sky, filled with stars that have guided travelers for millennia. Let this image inspire you to trust in your own inner guidance.

Affirmation: I trust in my own inner guidance, like the stars that have guided travelers for millennia, knowing that I am guided towards my true path.

Thought: The stars in the night sky, guiding travelers, teach us about the importance of trusting in our own inner guidance and intuition.

Focus: Trusting in inner guidance.

SACRED WISDOM – NATIVE AMERICAN MEDITATIONS, AFFIRMATIONS, AND REFLECTIONS

November 24

Meditation: Imagine the steady growth of a tree, each year adding new rings of strength and resilience. Let this image inspire you to grow steadily in your own life, adding layers of wisdom and experience.

Affirmation: I grow steadily in my life, like a tree adding new rings of strength and resilience each year, knowing that my experiences enrich and strengthen me.

Thought: The tree's steady growth teaches us about the value of growing steadily in our own lives, adding layers of wisdom and resilience with each passing year.

Focus: Steady growth and adding layers of wisdom.

November 25

Meditation: Visualize the quiet power of a sunrise, its light gradually illuminating the world. Let this image inspire you to approach new beginnings with a sense of hope and optimism.

Affirmation: I embrace new beginnings with hope and optimism, like the sunrise gradually illuminating the world, knowing that each day brings new possibilities.

Thought: The sunrise, with its quiet power, teaches us about the beauty and potential found in new beginnings, reminding us to approach them with a sense of hope and optimism.

Focus: Hope and optimism in new beginnings.

November 26

Meditation: Imagine the gentle dance of flames in a campfire, each flicker mesmerizing and unique. Let this image inspire you to embrace your own unique qualities and talents.

Affirmation: I embrace my uniqueness, like the dance of flames in a campfire, recognizing that my individuality is a source of strength and beauty.

Thought: The dance of flames in a campfire, each flicker different from the next, teaches us about the beauty and strength found in embracing our own unique qualities.

Focus: Embracing uniqueness and individuality.

SACRED WISDOM – NATIVE ANERICAN MEDITATIONS, AFFIRMATIONS, AND REFLECTIONS

November 27

Meditation: Picture the graceful flight of a butterfly, its wings carrying it effortlessly through the air. Let this image inspire you to move through life with grace and lightness.

Affirmation: I move through life with grace and lightness, like a butterfly fluttering through the air, embracing the beauty and joy of each moment.

Thought: The butterfly's graceful flight teaches us about the beauty of moving through life with grace and lightness, reminding us to savor each moment.

Focus: Grace and lightness in movement.

November 28

Meditation: Visualize the quiet strength of a mountain, standing tall and unyielding. Let this image inspire you to embody resilience and steadfastness in the face of challenges.

Affirmation: I embody strength and resilience, like a mountain standing tall and unyielding, facing challenges with grace and determination.

Thought: The mountain's quiet strength teaches us about the power of standing firm in the face of adversity, reminding us of our own inner strength.

Focus: Embodying strength and resilience.

November 29

Meditation: Picture the gentle touch of rain on the earth, nourishing and renewing life. Let this image inspire you to nurture and care for yourself, allowing for growth and renewal.

Affirmation: I nurture and care for myself, like the gentle rain nourishing the earth, allowing for growth and renewal in my mind, body, and spirit.

Thought: The rain's nurturing touch teaches us the importance of self-care and nourishment, reminding us to take time to nurture our own well-being.

Focus: Self-care and nurturing for growth.

SACRED WISDOM – NATIVE AMERICAN MEDITATIONS, AFFIRMATIONS, AND REFLECTIONS

November 30

Meditation: Reflect on the quiet wisdom of an elder, their words carrying the weight of experience. Let this image inspire you to seek wisdom and guidance from those who have walked before you.

Affirmation: I seek wisdom from those who have walked before me, honoring the experience and guidance of elders, knowing that their words carry valuable insights.

Thought: The wisdom of an elder, gained through a lifetime of experiences, teaches us the value of seeking guidance and learning from those who have lived longer.

Focus: Seeking wisdom from elders.

December 1

Meditation: Imagine the intricate patterns of frost on a window, each formation unique and beautiful. Let this natural artistry inspire appreciation for the beauty found in impermanence.

Affirmation: I appreciate the beauty of impermanence, like frost patterns on a window, recognizing the fleeting yet exquisite nature of life's moments.

Thought: Frost patterns, temporary and intricate, teach us about the beauty found in transient experiences, reminding us to cherish each moment as it comes.

Focus: Appreciating beauty in impermanence.

December 2

Meditation: Visualize the quiet resilience of a turtle, carrying its home on its back wherever it goes. Let this image inspire you to find strength and stability within yourself.

Affirmation: I carry my strength and stability within me, like a turtle carrying its home on its back, knowing that I am grounded and secure wherever I go.

Thought: The turtle's quiet strength teaches us about finding stability and security within ourselves, carrying our strength with us wherever life takes us.

Focus: Finding strength and stability within.

SACRED WISDOM – NATIVE ANERICAN MEDITATIONS, AFFIRMATIONS, AND REFLECTIONS

December 3

Meditation: Imagine the persistent growth of a vine, slowly but steadily climbing towards the sun. Let this image inspire you to pursue your goals with determination and perseverance.

Affirmation: I pursue my goals with determination and perseverance, like a vine climbing towards the sun, knowing that steady progress leads to great heights.

Thought: The vine's steady climb teaches us about the power of perseverance and the rewards that come from consistent effort towards our aspirations.

Focus: Determination and perseverance in pursuing goals.

December 4

Meditation: Picture the gentle sway of grass in the wind, each blade bending but not breaking. Let this image inspire flexibility and resilience in the face of life's challenges.

Affirmation: I am flexible and resilient, like the grass bending in the wind, adapting to life's challenges without losing my strength or resolve.

Thought: The grass's ability to bend without breaking teaches us about the value of flexibility and resilience in adapting to life's ever-changing circumstances.

Focus: Flexibility and resilience in facing challenges.

December 5

Meditation: Visualize the steady glow of a lighthouse on a stormy night, guiding ships to safety. Let this image inspire you to be a beacon of hope and guidance for others in difficult times.

Affirmation: I am a beacon of hope and guidance for others, like a lighthouse guiding ships to safety, offering light and reassurance in times of darkness.

Thought: The lighthouse's steady glow teaches us about the importance of being a source of light and guidance for others, offering hope and direction in their journeys.

Focus: Being a beacon of hope and guidance.

SACRED WISDOM – NATIVE ANERICAN MEDITATIONS, AFFIRMATIONS, AND REFLECTIONS

December 6

Meditation: Reflect on the gentle touch of snowflakes on the ground, each one unique and delicate. Let this image inspire you to appreciate the beauty of individuality and diversity.

Affirmation: I appreciate the beauty of individuality and diversity, like snowflakes falling to the ground, each one unique and exquisite in its own way.

Thought: The snowflake's uniqueness teaches us about the beauty found in individuality and diversity, reminding us to celebrate the differences that make us each special.

Focus: Appreciating individuality and diversity.

December 7

Meditation: Picture the quiet strength of a bear in hibernation, its rest a period of rejuvenation and preparation for the coming seasons. Let this image inspire you to embrace rest and renewal in your own life.

Affirmation: I embrace rest and renewal, like a bear in hibernation, knowing that periods of rest are essential for my well-being and growth.

Thought: The bear's hibernation teaches us about the importance of rest and renewal, reminding us to take time to rejuvenate our minds, bodies, and spirits.

Focus: Embracing rest and renewal.

December 8

Meditation: Imagine the vastness of the ocean, its depths holding mysteries and wonders beyond imagination. Let this image inspire you to explore the depths of your own inner being.

Affirmation: I explore the depths of my inner being, like the vast ocean holding mysteries and wonders, discovering new aspects of myself with each dive.

Thought: The ocean's vastness teaches us about the depth and complexity of our own inner beings, encouraging us to explore and discover our true selves.

Focus: Exploring the depths of inner being.

December 9

Meditation: Visualize the intricate patterns of a spider's web, each thread essential to its strength. Let this image inspire you to recognize the interconnectedness of all things.

Affirmation: I acknowledge my interconnectedness with all things, like the threads of a spider's web, knowing that my actions affect the greater whole.

Thought: The spider's web, intricately woven and interconnected, teaches us about the interdependence of all life and the impact of our actions on the world around us.

Focus: Recognizing the interconnectedness of all things.

December 10

Meditation: Imagine the gentle rustle of leaves in a forest, each tree swaying in harmony with the breeze. Let this image inspire you to find harmony and balance in your own life.

Affirmation: I find harmony and balance in my life, like the trees swaying in the forest, moving in harmony with the rhythms of life.

Thought: The forest's harmony, with each tree swaying in rhythm, teaches us about the importance of finding balance and moving in sync with the world around us.

Focus: Finding harmony and balance in life.

December 11

Meditation: Picture the intricate dance of a raindrop on a leaf, each movement deliberate and graceful. Let this image inspire you to move through life with intention and grace.

Affirmation: I move through life with intention and grace, like a raindrop dancing on a leaf, each movement deliberate and meaningful.

Thought: The raindrop's dance on a leaf teaches us about the beauty and power of moving through life with intention and grace, embracing each moment fully.

Focus: Moving with intention and grace.

SACRED WISDOM – NATIVE ANERICAN MEDITATIONS, AFFIRMATIONS, AND REFLECTIONS

December 12

Meditation: Visualize the silent strength of a rock formation, standing tall against the elements. Let this image inspire you to stand firm in your beliefs and values.

Affirmation: I stand firm in my beliefs and values, like a rock formation standing tall against the elements, unwavering in my convictions.

Thought: The rock formation's silent strength teaches us about the importance of standing firm in our beliefs and values, even in the face of adversity.

Focus: Standing firm in beliefs and values.

December 13

Meditation: Imagine the gentle touch of a breeze on your skin, its presence fleeting yet soothing. Let this image inspire you to appreciate life's fleeting moments of beauty.

Affirmation: I appreciate life's fleeting moments of beauty, like the gentle touch of a breeze on my skin, knowing that each moment is precious and fleeting.

Thought: The breeze's fleeting touch teaches us about the beauty found in transient experiences, reminding us to cherish each moment as it comes.

Focus: Appreciating life's fleeting moments.

December 14

Meditation: Reflect on the quiet resilience of a flower blooming in the desert, its beauty a testament to strength and perseverance. Let this image inspire you to bloom despite adversity.

Affirmation: I bloom despite adversity, like a flower in the desert, my beauty and strength shining through challenges and hardships.

Thought: The flower blooming in the desert teaches us about the power of resilience and perseverance, reminding us that beauty can thrive in the most unlikely of places.

Focus: Blooming despite adversity.

SACRED WISDOM – NATIVE ANERICAN MEDITATIONS, AFFIRMATIONS, AND REFLECTIONS

December 15

Meditation: Picture the vast expanse of the night sky, filled with stars that have guided travelers for millennia. Let this image inspire you to trust in your own inner guidance.

Affirmation: I trust in my own inner guidance, like the stars that have guided travelers for millennia, knowing that I am guided towards my true path.

Thought: The stars in the night sky, guiding travelers, teach us about the importance of trusting in our own inner guidance and intuition.

Focus: Trusting in inner guidance.

December 16

Meditation: Imagine the steady flow of a river, its waters carving a path through the landscape. Let this image inspire you to go with the flow of life, trusting in the journey.

Affirmation: I go with the flow of life, like a river carving its path, trusting in the journey and knowing that each twist and turn has purpose.

Thought: The river's steady flow teaches us about the importance of trusting in the journey of life, embracing its twists and turns with grace and acceptance.

Focus: Going with the flow and trusting in the journey.

December 17

Meditation: Imagine the quiet strength of a mountain, standing tall and majestic. Let this image inspire you to embody strength and resilience in the face of challenges.

Affirmation: I embody strength and resilience, like a mountain standing tall and unwavering, facing challenges with grace and determination.

Thought: The mountain's quiet strength teaches us about the power of standing firm in the face of adversity, reminding us of our own inner strength.

Focus: Embodying strength and resilience.

SACRED WISDOM – NATIVE AMERICAN MEDITATIONS, AFFIRMATIONS, AND REFLECTIONS

December 18

Meditation: Picture the gentle touch of rain on the earth, nourishing and renewing life. Let this image inspire you to nurture and care for yourself, allowing for growth and renewal.

Affirmation: I nurture and care for myself, like the gentle rain nourishing the earth, allowing for growth and renewal in my mind, body, and spirit.

Thought: The rain's nurturing touch teaches us the importance of self-care and nourishment, reminding us to take time to nurture our own well-being.

Focus: Self-care and nurturing for growth.

December 19

Meditation: Visualize the quiet power of a sunrise, its light gradually illuminating the world. Let this image inspire you to approach new beginnings with a sense of hope and optimism.

Affirmation: I embrace new beginnings with hope and optimism, like the sunrise gradually illuminating the world, knowing that each day brings new possibilities.

Thought: The sunrise, with its quiet power, teaches us about the beauty and potential found in new beginnings, reminding us to approach them with a sense of hope and optimism.

Focus: Hope and optimism in new beginnings.

December 20

Meditation: Imagine the steady growth of a tree, each year adding new rings of strength and resilience. Let this image inspire you to grow steadily in your own life, adding layers of wisdom and experience.

Affirmation: I grow steadily in my life, like a tree adding new rings of strength and resilience each year, knowing that my experiences enrich and strengthen me.

Thought: The tree's steady growth teaches us about the value of growing steadily in our own lives, adding layers of wisdom and resilience with each passing year.

Focus: Steady growth and adding layers of wisdom.

SACRED WISDOM – NATIVE ANERICAN MEDITATIONS, AFFIRMATIONS, AND REFLECTIONS

December 21

Meditation: Reflect on the intricate patterns of frost on a window, each formation unique and beautiful. Let this natural artistry inspire appreciation for the beauty found in impermanence.

Affirmation: I appreciate the beauty of impermanence, like frost patterns on a window, recognizing the fleeting yet exquisite nature of life's moments.

Thought: Frost patterns, temporary and intricate, teach us about the beauty found in transient experiences, reminding us to cherish each moment as it comes.

Focus: Appreciating beauty in impermanence.

December 22

Meditation: Visualize the quiet resilience of a turtle, carrying its home on its back wherever it goes. Let this image inspire you to find strength and stability within yourself.

Affirmation: I carry my strength and stability within me, like a turtle carrying its home on its back, knowing that I am grounded and secure wherever I go.

Thought: The turtle's quiet strength teaches us about finding stability and security within ourselves, carrying our strength with us wherever life takes us.

Focus: Finding strength and stability within.

December 23

Meditation: Imagine the persistent growth of a vine, slowly but steadily climbing towards the sun. Let this image inspire you to pursue your goals with determination and perseverance.

Affirmation: I pursue my goals with determination and perseverance, like a vine climbing towards the sun, knowing that steady progress leads to great heights.

Thought: The vine's steady climb teaches us about the power of perseverance and the rewards that come from consistent effort towards our aspirations.

Focus: Determination and perseverance in pursuing goals.

SACRED WISDOM – NATIVE ANERICAN MEDITATIONS, AFFIRMATIONS, AND REFLECTIONS

December 24

Meditation: Imagine the gentle rustle of leaves in a breeze, each movement a dance of life. Let this image inspire you to embrace the ever-changing nature of existence.

Affirmation: I embrace the ever-changing nature of existence, like leaves dancing in the breeze, moving with grace and acceptance.

Thought: The leaves' dance in the breeze teaches us about the beauty and inevitability of change, reminding us to embrace each moment as it comes.

Focus: Embracing the ever-changing nature of existence.

December 25

Meditation: Picture the intricate patterns of sand in a desert, shaped by the wind into unique formations. Let this image inspire you to see beauty in change and impermanence.

Affirmation: I see beauty in change and impermanence, like the intricate patterns of sand in a desert, knowing that each moment is fleeting yet beautiful in its own way.

Thought: The patterns of sand in a desert, shaped by the wind, teach us about the beauty found in impermanence and the ever-changing nature of life.

Focus: Seeing beauty in change and impermanence.

December 26

Meditation: Visualize the quiet wisdom of an elder, their words carrying the weight of experience. Let this image inspire you to seek guidance from those who have walked before you.

Affirmation: I seek guidance from elders and wise individuals, honoring their experience and wisdom, knowing that their insights are valuable.

Thought: The wisdom of an elder, gained through a lifetime of experiences, teaches us the value of seeking guidance and learning from those who have lived longer.

Focus: Seeking wisdom from elders and wise individuals.

SACRED WISDOM – NATIVE ANERICAN MEDITATIONS, AFFIRMATIONS, AND REFLECTIONS

December 27

Meditation: Reflect on the intricate dance of a raindrop on a window, each movement a reflection of its journey. Let this image inspire you to find beauty in simple moments.

Affirmation: I appreciate the beauty in simple moments, like the dance of a raindrop on a window, recognizing the magic in everyday experiences.

Thought: The raindrop's dance on a window teaches us about the beauty found in simple moments, reminding us to cherish the magic of everyday life.

Focus: Seeing the beauty in simple moments.

December 28

Meditation: Picture the gentle glow of a lantern in the darkness, its light guiding the way. Let this image inspire you to be a light for others in times of need.

Affirmation: I am a light for others in times of darkness, like a lantern guiding the way, offering warmth and guidance.

Thought: The lantern's gentle glow in the darkness teaches us about the importance of being a source of light and warmth for others, especially in their times of need.

Focus: Being a light for others in times of darkness.

December 29

Meditation: Imagine the vibrant colors of a sunset, painting the sky with beauty. Let this image inspire you to find beauty in endings and new beginnings.

Affirmation: I find beauty in endings and new beginnings, like the vibrant colors of a sunset, embracing the beauty of change.

Thought: The sunset's vibrant colors teach us about the beauty found in endings and new beginnings, reminding us that change can be a source of beauty and growth.

Focus: Finding beauty in endings and new beginnings.

SACRED WISDOM – NATIVE ANERICAN MEDITATIONS, AFFIRMATIONS, AND REFLECTIONS

December 30

Meditation: Visualize the quiet strength of a tree, its roots grounding it firmly in the earth. Let this image inspire you to find grounding and stability in your own life.

Affirmation: I am grounded and stable, like a tree with deep roots, finding strength and stability in the midst of life's challenges.

Thought: The tree's deep roots, anchoring it in the earth, teach us about the importance of finding grounding and stability in our own lives.

Focus: Finding grounding and stability.

December 31

Meditation: Picture the gentle flow of a river, its waters carving a path through the landscape. Let this image inspire you to go with the flow of life, trusting in the journey.

Affirmation: I go with the flow of life, like a river carving its path, trusting in the journey and knowing that each twist and turn has purpose.

Thought: The river's steady flow teaches us about the importance of trusting in the journey of life, embracing its twists and turns with grace and acceptance.

Focus: Going with the flow and trusting in the journey.

www.ingramcontent.com/pod-product-compliance
Lightning Source LLC
Chambersburg PA
CBHW050914160426
43194CB00011B/2396